John Guaspari

THE CUSTOMER CONNECTION

QUALITY
FOR THE REST OF US

Other AMACOM Books by John Guaspari

I KNOW IT WHEN I SEE IT:
A MODERN FABLE ABOUT QUALITY
(now available in paperback).

THEORY WHY:
IN WHICH THE BOSS SOLVES THE RIDDLE OF QUALITY

A video based on THE CUSTOMER CONNECTION is also available. For information about the video, THE QUALITY CONNECTION, and other innovative videos on quality featuring John Guaspari please call the Video Customer Service Center at 800-225-3215 (in MA call 617-926-4600) or write them at 9 Galen Street, Watertown, MA 02172.

John Guaspari

THE CUSTOMER CONNECTION

QUALITY FOR THE REST OF US

amacom

American Management Association

This book is available at a special
discount when ordered in bulk quantities.
For information, contact Special Sales Department,
AMACOM, a division of American Management Association,
135 West 50th Street, New York, NY 10020.

Library of Congress Cataloging-in-Publication Data

Guaspari, John.
    The customer connection.

    1. Quality of products—Miscellanea.
I. Title.
HD38.G765   1988   658.5′62   88-47695
ISBN 0-8144-5837-8
ISBN 0-8144-7758-5 (pbk.)

First AMACOM paperback edition 1991.

Printing number

10   9   8   7   6   5   4   3   2   1

For
Joanna

Preface

*T*his is not a book about the techniques of quality assurance and quality control, so if that's what you're looking for, you'd be better off somewhere else. Understand, that's not because mastery of such techniques isn't important. In fact, it's absolutely essential. No serious, sustainable effort at achieving quality improvement will succeed without the vigilant application of the teachings and methodologies offered by the true experts in the field: Deming, Juran, Crosby, Feigenbaum, and the rest.

But I'm not going to write about those things for the simple reason that I'm not an expert in quality assurance or quality control. I'm a marketing guy. My formal training was as an engineer—an aerospace/mechanical engineer to be specific. I studied aerospace engineering as an undergraduate student and as a graduate student. Then, having spent so much time—and probably more to the point, so much of my parents' money—on that education, I felt that I owed it to my parents to try to be an engineer, which I was for two years. At which point I felt I owed it to the American flying public to stop, which I also did. I then spent the next eleven years in various positions in marketing and marketing support and marketing management for a number of companies in the Boston area.

I came to the topic of quality about five or six years ago. The company I was working for was in the process of introducing a new line of what it called "quality management systems." Essentially, these were central computers that would "pull" process test data off a manufacturing floor, apply some smart quality management software to those raw data, and then turn them into useful management information. As the manager of corporate marketing programs, I had some responsibility for the "get a clear, compelling, effective message out there" portion of the marketing task.

To meet that responsibility, I immersed myself in the topic of quality. I read whatever I could get my hands on, attended seminars and training programs, talked to customers, and spoke with experts and nonexperts in the field of quality. You get the picture. One of the things that quickly emerged from my study was this: According to all the quality experts, if efforts at improving quality are going to be successful, they cannot be viewed as the responsibility of "the quality department," those technical specialists working out of some secluded corner of the building, stereotyped as wearing white lab coats and carrying clipboards and calipers and stopwatches everywhere they go. Rather, quality efforts must be viewed as *everybody's* responsibility: all employees, all functions, at all levels in the organization.

Now that made (and makes) perfect sense. But when you take a step back from the insight that "quality is everybody's job" and look at where that insight is usually found, you begin to get an inkling of the problem. Because that insight usually appears somewhere in the first ten pages of a 962-page textbook on quality control. Or it's expressed in the first thirty minutes of an intensive, week-long management seminar. Or it appears in the first of a series of a dozen, hour-long training videotapes. In other words, everybody must understand and embrace—"take ownership of," to use the vernacular—the quality message. But everybody isn't going to hear it, because everybody isn't going to read the 962-page book, or attend the management seminar, or view the videotapes. Still, the core of the message must get through to *all* those in the organization—all people, all functions, all levels—regardless of their experience or training in the topic of quality as a formal discipline.

So the question becomes: What to do? How do you get that core message through to everyone without suggesting that everyone sign up for a tour of duty in the quality department, a suggestion that in itself is contradicted by the "quality is not the responsibility of the quality department" dictum of that core message?

It was in trying to come up with an answer that, in 1985, I wrote a book called *I Know It When I See It: A Modern Fable About Quality*. It was an attempt to widely communicate some of the basic truths about quality in a simple, entertaining way. That being the case, I established two inviolable standards for the book.

First of all, it had to be readable in under an hour. I circulated early drafts to willing readers and asked them to be sure to keep track of how long it took them to read the entire manuscript. Early readers averaged out at about ninety minutes. Too long. I made some cuts. Seventy minutes was the norm. Still too long. It was only after two or three more rounds of revisions that I got things down comfortably under the one-hour mark. My hope was that that would enable a quality believer to hand the book to a potential convert and say: "Take an hour out of your life and read this. If nothing else, you might get a chuckle or two out of it."

My second standard was that, although I wanted to write a story about a company that was experiencing quality problems, I didn't want readers to be able to say: "But we're not in that business." So I invented an organization called Punctuation Inc., the world's leading maker and seller of punctuation marks, whose market dominance came to be threatened by a competitor called Process Inc. I figured that a product line of periods and commas and semicolons was so obviously a metaphor for real products that it would be harder for readers to deny at least some level of relevance to their business. It seems to have worked, since over the past three years I have had people from every conceivable kind of business— manufacturing and service, high tech and low tech, public and private—say to me: "When I read *I Know It When I See It*, I knew you had to have written it about us!" That was very gratifying, as was the acceptance of the sequel, *Theory Why: In Which the Boss Solves the Riddle of Quality*.

Some readers, though, weren't so enchanted. They thought that those two books about Punctuation Inc. trivialized the issues. Implicit in their objections (and in some cases explicit) was the notion that I was somehow suggesting that quality problems could be solved merely by spinning a charming little tale or two, and that there was no need to worry about the rigorous knowledge and application of quality techniques. (For the record, this book is not about Punctuation Inc. or the punctuation industry.)

Well, the fact is that organizations do need to know and apply such techniques, and to do so they need a few people who are functional experts in the field of quality and a much, much larger number of people to follow the lead of those functional experts. It was for the inexpert many (i.e., people like me) and not the expert few that those books were written.

That's also what this book is for: to help get the quality message out in a way that's of interest to "the rest of us." (For an elaboration on this point, see the brief section entitled "Before We Begin," which starts on page 1.) There's not a lot of technical detail; as I said earlier, there are plenty of places to go for that. Rather, it's intended to frame the issue of quality in simple, basic, and—above all—*identifiable* terms. Thanks for reading it. I hope that it delivers the value for which you paid.

John Guaspari
April 1988
WALPOLE, MASSACHUSETTS

Acknowledgments

What follow are the acknowledgments as they appeared in the first edition of this book. Although the passage of two years has caused the specifics of some of the references to be dated, what hasn't changed is my level of gratitude toward those cited. That being the case, I have decided to leave those acknowledgments as they first appeared. The one difference that I would like to call explicit attention to stems from the fact that about a year ago I joined the consulting firm of Rath & Strong. And during that year's time, I have learned more about Total Quality and—more importantly—how to make it happen in the push and pull of organizational life than I had in my previous 40 years on this planet. For that I am most obliged to all of my Rath & Strong colleagues.

If I believe what I have written in this book, then I must begin with a general acknowledgment of the people who have bought my books and films, attended my seminars, and sat through my speeches. That is to say, I must acknowledge my customers. I thank them, obviously, for purchasing those products. But I also thank them for giving me the opportunity to test some ideas and the feedback necessary to refine such ideas to the point where this book came to be written.

Now to a few, more specific acknowledgments.

I am indebted to Ron Mallis, Vice-President, Corporate Product Development for the American Management Association, and the editor of this book. Along with those more formal designations, Ron is also a good listener and a good friend. With the confidence that he has shown in me and his willingness to take risks with me over the past four years, he has done more for me professionally than anyone I know, and I am very grateful to him.

I am also grateful to Mindy Somers, who works with Ron in AMA's Boston office. Mindy deals with our seminar customers every day and in so doing she provides us with a built-in standard for "how to do it right." When I visit a customer site and things have been handled so smoothly as to be invisible to that customer—which is exactly as it should be—my one regret is that in doing her job so well, Mindy in effect hides her contributions to our efforts. Well, they're a little less hidden now, and I thank her. A lot.

I spent seven and a half sometimes exhilarating, sometimes frustrating, but always interesting years working for GenRad, a maker of automatic test equipment and quality management systems. In that time I learned from many people, two of whom I would like to acknowledge here.

As my boss and then Vice-President of Marketing, Bob Anderson (he's now GenRad's President and CEO) gave me the opportunity and the encouragement to spread my wings and try some new approaches to moving an organization toward a deeper commitment to customer satisfaction. The value of that on-the-job training is surpassed only by the value of having had a chance to work with and know a man of Bob's caliber.

Officially, John Ferrie was GenRad's Director of Training and Development. Unofficially, he was the guy who would, at semi-regular intervals, give me a kick in the rear end and tell me to stop rationalizing about why I couldn't do certain things and just, for crying out loud, do them! It was a lesson much needed and, I hope, well learned.

Finally...

It is customary to thank one's spouse for invariably being "tireless in reading through the manuscript, turning it into serviceable English, and transforming my chicken-scrawled notations into a neatly typed and presentable format." Unfortunately, I did the typing, I got better grades in grammar than my wife did, and she has probably only just now gotten around to reading the manuscript. Gail's sole contribution to the writing of this book was this:

She made (and makes) each day better than the last one. When you're in the middle of a year-long project, that counts for quite a lot.

My son, Michael, is five years old. A few weeks ago, someone asked him that age-old question: "What do you want to be when you grow up?" Michael said: "When I grow up, I don't want to be anything—just like Daddy." This is one of the drawbacks of working out of one's home. It is also one of those "out of the mouths of babes" moments that helps keep things in perspective. For that, and for countless other exasperatingly insightful moments, I thank Michael.

My daughter, Joanna, is one year old. Being one, she hasn't said anything insightful yet. (That's not because she hasn't had any insights yet, but because she hasn't *said* anything yet.) Being Joanna, she deserves an acknowledgment. So, thanks Jo.

Contents

"The latest studies seem to show a strong correlation between our troubles and our customers' perceptions that doing business with us is like throwing money down a rathole."

Dick Vieira/John Guaspari

Before We Begin

*W*hat follows here is the sort of thing usually found in the preface of a book. But: (a) not everybody reads prefaces; (b) an awful lot of this book talks about the importance of properly "setting expectations"; so (c) in the interest of practicing what I preach, I decided to put this right up front in order to make sure that your expectations for what you are about to read are accurately set. Because if I've done my job right, you will probably find this book to be different from other books you've read on the topic of quality. Not necessarily better or worse (which is for you to judge), but different.

The connection between quality and customer satisfaction is a very serious topic. And in the main essays that begin each chapter of this book, I have tried to make my points in a straightforward, expository way. Nothing new in that.

It's in the other material that the differences occur. Because in the other material I have tried to deal with serious subject matters and make a serious case in a decidedly nonserious way. My intention here is to give you a "breather" between the more analytical sections as well as to provide you with a variety of new communications tools that might be of help in getting the customer satisfaction/quality message across in your business organizations.

Please understand that although my objectives are quite serious, humor can sometimes be used to help an argument cut more cleanly but with a little less sting. Hence the cartoon on page xvi. And the quizzes at the end of several of the case studies in the book. And the verses that appear at the end of each chapter. And the "Ask Mr. Quality!" and "More Ask Mr. Quality!" advice columns.

The piece entitled "The Obligatory Section About 'Why Japan Is Better at Quality Than We Are,' " which starts on page 14, is another case in point. I have very little patience with those who would argue (read: rationalize) that the Japanese possess some sort of *fundamental* advantage in the area of quality, and I have tried here to lampoon that notion. In "This Too Shall Pass: A Tragicomedy in One Act," which begins on page 179, I have tried to raise some serious issues about the running of organizational quality improvement efforts in what I hope is an entertaining—and effective—way. In "The Big Game," starting on page 206, I've tried to have some fun with certain serious reservations I have about the notion of the so-called "internal customer." And so on throughout the book.

Why bring all this up here? Because these materials *are* different, and expectations *do* need to be set. If, for you, this discussion amounts to overstating the obvious and is therefore unnecessary, my apologies. But I'd rather run the risk of overstating the obvious than leave unsaid something that needs to be said.

Now to the business at hand.

1

How Has "Quality" Gotten Such a Bad Name?

I was the manager of corporate marketing programs for a $200-million-plus Route 128 electronics company, a corporate staff position reporting to the Vice-President of Marketing. Phil was a manager in the company's quality department, a corporate staff position reporting to the Vice-President of Quality. We were scheduled to meet to discuss "quality in the marketing function."

Now, I realize that the thought of two corporate staffers meeting summons up strong reactions in many people, particularly in "operations" people (or as operations people would describe it, "in people with *real* jobs"). Optimists among them might take solace in the fact that "while those two staffers are together they'll only be bothering *each other*." Pessimists, on the other hand, would conclude darkly that "no good can come of such a collaboration." The fact that both assessments usually turn out to be right is the subject for another book.

In any case, the bickering didn't concern me. For one thing, it "goes with the territory" of being in a staff position. Or as the saying goes, "If you can't stand the ivory, get out of the tower." For another thing, it was becoming clearer every day that quality was rightly taking its place as an issue of bedrock strategic importance. It could no longer be treated in apple-pie-and-motherhood fashion, trotted out at the annual Lip Service to Quality! pageant and then left to gather dust until next year. No longer was the language of quality the language of "inherent goodness" and "virtue" and "excellence in spirit or kind." Now quality was described in real down-and-dirty, substantive terms like "profitability," "productivity," "market share," "competitive position"—even "survival."

Clearly my colleague Phil and I were meeting to discuss a matter of the highest importance. I knew that Phil was a very competent, committed professional who could provide me with valuable counsel and assistance. (Have I mentioned that one of the corporate marketing programs under my responsibility was designed to help improve the quality of the marketing function throughout the corporation? In other words, my corporate interest in our quality efforts was liberally seasoned with self-interest.) I wanted to cooperate with Phil and was looking forward to our meeting. As I remember, it went something like the following.

✳ ✳ ✳

PHIL: John, thanks for giving me some time to talk to you about quality as it relates to the marketing function.

ME: I can't think of an area where there's more quality progress to be made than in marketing. Having the right product at the right price in the right place at the right time—the possibilities are mind-boggling! You're really providing an invaluable service to the corporation with your work, Phil. I know it's a tough job, and I'm only too happy to help you in any way that I can.

PHIL: That's nice to hear. You can't imagine the kind of resistance that I run into in other departments. People think I'm out to get them. They don't understand that major benefits are to be gained by improving quality in all functions, and that by doing my job I can make their jobs easier.

ME: Well, you won't get any of that stuff from me.

PHIL: Glad to hear it. So why don't we get on with it?

ME: Let's do it!

PHIL: OK. First of all, John, can you help me get a feeling for what the cost of quality is? Actually, I probably ought to say "the cost of *unquality*"! Quality doesn't cost anything. It's making mistakes and then fixing them that costs!

ME: Absolutely! You don't have to convince me of that!

PHIL: Good! So, can you help me identify the cost of unquality in, say, producing a product brochure?

ME: Er, I suppose so, Phil. Just what did you have in mind?

PHIL: I did a little homework and talked to some of the people who get involved in those projects. And some interesting things came up.

ME: For example?

PHIL: For example, my understanding is that when we produce a brochure, we buy the typesetting from an outside vendor. Is that right?

ME: Yup.

PHIL: But when the typeset copy comes in from the vendor, it doesn't usually go straight to the next stage of production—to whattayacallit?

ME: Mechanicals?

PHIL: Yeah, mechanicals. It doesn't usually go straight into mechanicals, does it?

ME: Well, it should, but there are almost always changes to be made at that point.

PHIL: Do we pay extra for that?

ME: Do you know anyone who runs a charity typesetting house? If you do, let me know. We could save a lot of money.

PHIL: So if we were more careful and made sure that there would be no changes to the copy—in other words, if we "designed the quality in" rather than repairing it after the mistakes were made—we could eliminate that waste. *That's a cost of unquality!* Can you help me get some figures as to what those costs were last year?

ME: Uh, I suppose so, Phil, but—

PHIL: And if you could break those figures out on a project-by-project basis, charging them all back to the appropriate product lines, and then aggregate all product lines and break this out on a month-by-month and then quarter-by-quarter basis, that would be a big help.

ME: I guess so, but it seems to me that our time might be better spent by looking into other areas.

PHIL: Ah, ah, ah—I thought you were one of us, John! That's the same sort of thing I hear everywhere I go: "Don't look at my department. Look at the other guy's!"

ME: No, Phil, don't get me wrong. I'm not saying we should look at other departments. I'm merely suggesting that we look elsewhere within the marketing function. I think we have bigger fish to fry than counting up changes made to brochure copy.

PHIL: If you can't measure it, you can't manage it. We've got to "count up" things, as you put it, and attach a dollar figure to them if we're going to be able to do anything about them.

ME: I don't disagree. I'm just questioning the "them" that we're talking about, that's all.

PHIL: OK. So that we don't get hung up on this one item, why don't we move on to something else? After all, we're allies in this quality battle, right?!?

ME: Right!

PHIL: Right. So tell me, John, are there any other problem areas that come to mind with the production of brochures?

ME: Brochures?

PHIL: Yes, brochures.

ME: Well, I bring this up only because it's something that we were dealing with just yesterday. It's our practice to list all our sales offices—worldwide—on the back cover of our brochures. That can be a real headache.

PHIL: How so?

ME: Because if that information is going to be of any use to anyone, it has to include things like each office's phone number and mailing address.

PHIL: That doesn't seem like such a big deal.

ME: It wouldn't be, except that the company is growing so fast that new offices are opening all the time, and old offices seem to be constantly moving into bigger facilities. It's a real nightmare trying to keep that information up to date. Don't get me wrong—I'm not complaining that the company is doing so well. It's a nice problem to have to face. But it *is* a problem.

PHIL: I see. So what happens when people get a brochure that has outdated information?

ME: Sometimes they call in here to headquarters asking how they can reach their local office. Some people get really upset: "I called the old number and it was disconnected! Are you people abandoning me out here?!?" But we take a little time to explain the situation to them and put them at ease.

PHIL: How much time do you take?

ME: Excuse me?

PHIL: Well, if you could tell me how much time such a call would take—on average, of course; we don't want to pretend to a false precision in these figures—then I could multiply it by the average salary of the person who takes the call, and that would give us a figure for another cost of unquality.

ME: I guess it would.

PHIL: There! Now we're making progress! Working together to improve quality and realizing some tangible, measurable benefits in the process! Tell me, because of the mistakes made in printing the addresses on brochures, do payments ever get made to the wrong address?

ME: That might happen, but I have a problem with your characterizing them as "mistakes made in printing the addresses."

PHIL: You know, it would be good to know how long, on average, payments were delayed because of the incorrect addresses. The interest might add up to something appreciable. There's another cost of unquality.

ME: And since we're on the subject, it's also incorrect to call the changes made to the brochure copy "mistakes." They were revisions made to the copy between the time it was approved and the time the type was set.

PHIL: Let's not quibble over semantics. I wonder, could you work up the figures—nothing elaborate—on the frequency with which payments are made to the wrong address, correlate that to the total amount invoiced, and then multiply it by the prevailing interest rate over the time period in question—on a per diem basis, of course?

ME: No.

PHIL: No?

ME: No. Look, Phil. I want to improve marketing quality as much as you do. God knows there's money to be made by doing that. Hell, I've got responsibility for the company's "marketing quality program," so my rear end is on the line, too. But I want to talk about how we can get better at understanding our marketplace, what it needs, and how we can deliver it. And you come in here and get all over my case about mistakes in our brochures and expect me to spend my time digging through back issues of the *Wall Street Journal* to find out what interest rates have been for the past six months!

PHIL: A quarterly average would be good enough, I suppose.

ME: Phil! You're not listening! And you weren't listening before when I told you that those weren't mistakes; they were the inevitable outcome of trying to do business in the constant state of flux that we find ourselves in.

PHIL: Those "inevitable outcomes" are costing us a lot of money. We could find out just how much and make better use of our assets if someone would be willing to take the time to do a little research.

ME: You want someone to do the research? Then go talk to the product planning people! They're the ones who don't know their assets from their elbows and keep changing the product specs on us. That's why we have to change the brochure copy after the type has already been set. And then when you're finished with those bozos, you can talk to the business planning people. If they could see further ahead than a week from next Tuesday, maybe they'd know enough not to move our sales offices into buildings that we've already outgrown before the ink is dry on the lease!

PHIL: Now, we won't get anywhere by pointing fingers.

ME: Sure we will. We'll get to the end of this meeting. See, it worked! We've just arrived!

PHIL: Are you telling me to leave?

ME: Yes, Phil, yes! L-E-A-V-E! There, have I said it clearly enough? Because I realize that if I'm careless and you have to ask me again what I really mean, we'll incur another cost of unquality. Then we'll have to calculate the incremental prolongation of our conversation and multiply it by our salaries—on a minute-by-minute basis, of course.

PHIL: John, don't you think you're behaving rather unprofessionally?

ME: I was wondering, should we do a present-value calculation? After all, when you factor in the time value of money, a fixed salary at the beginning of this meeting is worth more than the same fixed salary at the end of this meeting.

PHIL: Frankly, John, I'm surprised. I'm used to getting this kind of treatment from other people, but I thought it would be different here. I thought you understood the importance of quality and wanted to do something about it.

ME: Well, I guess you were wrong, Phil. I guess I had you fooled. I guess I've had everybody fooled, because, you see, I really *don't* give a damn about quality. Just call me old good-enough-to-get-by John. Yup, just give me some work to do and I'll hand in any old piece of crap, as long as it's "good enough." In a strange sort of way, I'm glad you caught on to my game, Phil. Because an attitude like mine is a sort of cancer that can quickly spread through an organization. If you catch it fast enough, you can do something about it. Let it go unchecked and, well, hey—I don't have to tell you that it's important to smoke out sources of potential problems and eliminate them. You're in the quality department! I guess you recognized all those mistakes on the product brochures for what they really were: a cry for help. I and the rest of the corporation are forever in your debt. Now, if you'll excuse me, Phil, I'd like to pick up the pieces of what's left of my once promising career and see what I can do to make a new beginning.

PHIL: OK, but John?

ME: Yes, Phil.

PHIL: Does this mean that you won't be doing up that analysis on the costs involved in responding to the incorrect addresses on the brochures?

ME: No, Phil. And besides—you wouldn't want me to do that analysis anyway. Unless, of course, you'd be willing to accept any old piece of garbage.

PHIL: Well, no. That wouldn't do.

ME: I didn't think so. Good-bye, Phil.

PHIL: Good-bye, John.

✳ ✳ ✳

Remember, I said the meeting went "something like" that dialogue. Literally speaking, yes, the scene is a bit of an exaggeration. But it is *impressionistically* accurate. That is, I was left with an overall sense of frustration, of feeling that I was on the hot seat, of defensiveness, and ultimately of exasperation with the whole quality improvement effort. I felt that I was as motivated and committed as anyone to the success of the company—and, to that end, the need to manage quality. I resented the insinuation (real or imagined; as a practical matter it makes no difference) that I somehow wasn't.

The point here is not to indict Phil. The slight exaggerations (all right, all right: gross distortions) in this scene notwithstanding, Phil was—and remains—a bright, competent, and thoroughly committed manager. He was not out to "keep tabs on me." He wasn't trying to make my life more difficult. But somehow, for whatever reason, he managed to alienate someone who should have been a strong ally, to turn what should have been a collaborative situation into a contentious one. Understand that it's not terribly important that Phil had alienated *me*. God knows I hadn't covered myself with glory during our exchange. But it is important that, by Phil's own account, he had gotten a similar reaction everywhere. If he encountered that reaction in me—someone in a corporate staff position, someone who was theoretically insulated from a lot of the day-to-day pressures that can make the implementation of a long-term quality improvement effort so difficult—imagine what Phil came up against in dealing with, say, the director of manufacturing at the end of the month or the end of the quarter. Not for the squeamish to consider.

So where's the problem? What went wrong? How did "this quality stuff" get such a bad name? Appropriately (and, I suppose, ironically) the answer comes from the quality orthodoxy itself, which holds that assessing blame is not the issue. (It wasn't Phil's fault; he was just doing his job. It wasn't my fault either; I was raising some perfectly justifiable points—albeit a tad emotionally at times.) Rather, the unquality in question is the inevitable result of "the way things are done," not the people doing the work. Or to use the quality vernacular, it's a "process problem," not a "people problem."

So let's take a look at how all this came about. Up until

fairly recently (and the definition of "fairly recently" will vary from industry to industry and company to company), the issue of quality was dealt with in a sort of "transcendent" way, not as a serious business issue. But things have changed. (I will here refer to the reason for that change as "the J-word" and leave it at that.) Now people realize that quality is a very serious business issue indeed, arguably the most serious business issue (arguably, in fact, the *only* business issue). They realize that quality must be intensively studied and extensively managed. They realize that quality must be viewed as the responsibility of everyone in every department and not just the responsibility of the quality assurance (QA) or quality control (QC) department. And they've begun to go at it with a vengeance by applying the thoroughly proven and manifestly powerful quality techniques and methodologies developed by the true masters in the field like Deming et al.

All of that represents significant progress. But in the process (there's that word again) of applying those techniques and methodologies, it can be easy to lose sight of an important fact: Yes, quality is the responsibility of everyone in the organization, but not everyone in the organization wants to be a QA/QC professional. Moreover, not everyone in the organization *needs* to be a QA/QC professional.

I think that's the point on which Phil and I began to come apart. As a QA/QC professional, he knew that his objectives were purely analytical and not judgmental. He could look at a situation and very quickly and insightfully zero in on a problem. He could do that because that's what he was trained to do, what he did all the time. And because that's what he did all the time, he was able to bring to the task the kind of professional detachment that was required.

But the application of QA/QC techniques was not what I did all the time. I had not been trained to implement quality methodologies. So my reaction was anything but detached. It was personal, emotional, defensive, and maybe even more than a little childish. And the point is: Such personal/emotional/defensive/childish reactions are an inevitable result of taking someone out of context and suddenly immersing him in "all this quality stuff."

"But," some QA/QC professionals may argue, "people have just got to understand that quality is of critical importance to the well-being of this organization. They've just got to learn to deal with it."

And that's true—up to a point. An analogy might be helpful here. Consider the current fitness boom. More and more people are paying more and more attention to health, to "wellness." That's all to the good. But it doesn't follow that more and more people necessarily have a burning desire to enroll in medical school. What's happened is that, armed with a better overall understanding of and sensitivity to the workings of their bodies, people are better attuned to knowing when (and whether) to call an expert (i.e., a doctor) for assistance. The doctor is steeped in the techniques and methodologies of the medical profession; the patient has a better feel for "what to be sensitive to" and what it might mean; and the doctor-patient combination, net, functions together more effectively— the *process* functions more effectively.

I care a great deal about quality on the job. I have absolutely no desire to be a QA/QC professional. There is no conflict in those statements. But what's needed to make the relationship between the QA/QC professional and the average employee like me work effectively (i.e., this "doctor-patient relationship") is that I be similarly armed with a better overall understanding of and sensitivity to the workings of the organization. That I know what to monitor—what the quality equivalents are to my weight, my blood pressure, my temperature. That I know what to do in response to those readings—whether I should take two aspirin, call the doctor, call an ambulance, or call the coroner.

What's important is that I, as an average employee—and by average I mean the person not formally a part of the QA/QC department at any level in any function—have a better *overall sense* of what this quality stuff is all about. There are ways to achieve that without "enrolling in medical school," and those ways must be part of the *process* of quality improvement.

The Obligatory Section About "Why Japan Is Better at Quality Than We Are"

To be honest, I really didn't want to write this section. But people told me that I had to, that it's a rule that books about quality have to have something in them about the Japanese approach and why it's so much better. What's more, there's another rule that says you have to reduce things to nice, convenient lists containing ten items. Well, I want to play by the rules, but I'm telling you right now that I'm going to have a hard time stretching this section out to ten items, so consider yourself forewarned.

1. *Japanese workers are guaranteed lifetime employment.*

Whenever you talk about quality and Japan you're supposed to make a big deal about this. It's another rule. But to be honest, I don't think this is a very big factor at all. In fact, to be *really* honest, I don't even think that Japanese workers actually get lifetime employment. It's just that when you go to work and spend all your time talking about quality it *seems* like a lifetime, that's all. So don't worry about this one.

2. *Japanese management style encourages commitment to quality.*

Another legislated requirement. But unlike the business about lifetime employment, this one happens to be true. Yes, it is that Japanese style which leads to such insightful management pronouncements as: "We'd better work on this some more. If we build it this way, it won't work properly. Then people will stop buying our products and that promise of lifetime employment you've heard so much about won't be worth bupkus."

3. *George Steinbrenner is an American.*

All the experts will tell you that achieving quality is a long, painstaking process. It calls for steadiness, professionalism, calmness, predictability. Substituting rationalism for emotion. Sublimating your ego for the betterment of the whole. Fostering teamwork over individualism. After you have mastered those requirements, the experts say, you can realize the riches and benefits that quality can provide. You can spend years preaching that gospel to the people in your organization. Then they see Steinbrenner on the six o'clock news, figure that guy made millions by acting the way he does, and start looking for shortcuts.

4. *The Japanese realize that quality is too important not to have some fun with it.*

One of the most important breakthroughs in cost reduction stemming from quality improvement is the idea that you really shouldn't keep a lot of inventory hanging around the factory. If you run things right, materials don't have to be delivered until the moment they're actually needed in production. In the United States, this is known as "just-in-time" inventory. Notice how serious-sounding that name is, implying a sort of perils-of-Pauline brinksmanship. It used to be much nicer and friendlier in the old days, when manufacturers would keep a little extra on hand to help deal with unforeseen problems— the not much talked about but widely practiced "just-in-case" approach to inventory management. The Japanese word for just-in-time is *kanban*, which is a lot more fun to say than just-in-time. I'm not sure why, but I think this probably makes a difference.

5. *Japan is a skinny island (actually, an archipelago).*

All the residents of Japan have lived their entire lives within a stone's throw of the sea. So it's no big deal to them. It just isn't. As a result, they don't waste a lot of time and energy romanticizing about "life amidst the briny blue." The way I figure it, we've got millions of people in places like Kansas and the Dakotas wondering what the ocean must be like when they could be boning up on the latest advances in quality. We'd be a lot better off if we would just adopt a more mature, blasé attitude about this ocean business.

6. *The Japanese are better able to deal with the warp and woof of life as we approach the third millennium* A.D.

I have no idea what this means. But I figure that this list gives me a chance to be the first one to use the phrase "warp and woof of life as we approach the third millennium A.D."

7. *The Japanese don't cook their fish.*

They use this extra time to learn more about quality. (They really do.) We get a little extra time, we'll blow it perfecting an Elvis impersonation.

8. *All VCRs are made in Japan.*

An especially paranoid friend of mine told me that he read someplace that all VCRs now contain some sort of special microchip that causes subliminal messages to appear on your TV screen while you're playing a tape. Things like: "You will never be able to overcome the quality advantage held by your honorable Japanese trading partners, so just eat some more fried fish and don't worry about it." And: "Seems to me your Elvis could use a little work, don't ya think?" Sounds pretty insidious. I don't really believe it, but my friend asked me to pass it along, so I did.

9. If we're not very good at something, then it really can't be very important.

This is a pervasive attitude in America and explains both why we've never really taken this quality stuff very seriously and the ratings for televised soccer games.

10. Americans will pay good money for books and seminars about quality in order to be exposed to insights such as "Good is good, better is even better, and best is best of all," "It's cheaper to do things one time than two times," and "Customers tend to buy things that work before they buy things that don't."

This observation is one of the more interesting things about the warp and woof of life in the United States as we approach the third millenium A.D.

The Quantity
of Quality (and Vice Versa)

If quality is an entity
Available in limited quantity,
But the policy of the powers-that-be
Is to increase the quantity of quality,
So that the total cost of the entity
Is much higher than they'd want it to be,
Does it become a policy fallacy
To strive for quantity quality?

If quality is an entity
That apparently just isn't meant to be,
Since the measures taken so skillfully
Lead to measurements made so unwillfully,
Does that, in practicality,
As theory collides with reality,
Raise some serious questions of policy
As to the overall quality of quantity?

2

The Toughest Things About Quality

*A*chieving quality is difficult. If it weren't, more people would do it, and they don't, so it is.

For one thing, dealing with quality means facing up to implied criticism with how you're doing your job. "Are you trying to tell me that I, who toils for forty, no fifty, no sixty-plus hours each week!—I, my dear mother's own child, can actually do my job *better?*"

As a matter of fact, yes. And there's no reason that such a notion should be offensive to anyone since it is merely the logical equivalent of saying, "Nobody's perfect." But offense is often taken, and a perfectly reasonable statement of fact ("You have some responsibility for the level of quality produced") can get distorted into a most unreasonable personal indictment and assessment of blame ("Our quality problems are all your fault!"). That wouldn't seem to be the subtlest distinction to keep a hold on, but in the push and pull of organizational life, with so many demands on everyone's time and energy and good nature, people get defensive. That's ultimately wasteful, counterproductive, and self-defeating. It's also perfectly natural, human, and understandable, and one of the reasons that quality is such a tough nut to crack.

Another thing about quality: I don't know about you, but if I've got a busy job, and I have to deal with thirty-seven things every day, and I know that there isn't enough time in the day to do the things I already have to do, the last thing I need is for somebody to come along and give me nine *more* things to do on top of the other thirty-seven. I know that improving quality will, net, save me time and effort. And I know that it will make me more productive. And I know that it's a "good thing" to do. But any way you slice it, making all those measurements and doing all that analysis and sitting in all those meetings that "the quality people" are talking about sure as hell looks to me like *extra work*. And I don't need any more to do! (One director of quality tried to address that problem by exhorting people with the slogan: "Steal time for quality!" I give him an A+ for honesty, a B+ for effort, and an F for salesmanship.)

A third difficulty with quality is the extent to which improving it gets translated into a need to *change*. You don't have to read this book to know that "change is painful," that people (and, by extension, organizations) resist change. This difficulty goes hand in glove with difficulty number one: the tendency for people to react defensively. We go to great lengths to depersonalize our quality efforts by (correctly) focusing on the need to adopt a process orientation, saying things like: "Quality problems are not caused by the *people* who do the work. Quality problems are *process* problems. They are caused by *the way* the work gets done." You don't have to have a Ph.D. in quality control to know that what comes next is "So we are going to *change* the way we do things around here!" Do you think people will be inclined to charge up the hill behind that banner? Neither do I.

Another difficulty is that quality improvement is a decidedly unglamorous undertaking. It's not a matter of finding "the secret," applying it once, and then sitting back to watch the sun shine and hear the birds sing, forevermore. It's more a matter of finding a thousand and one painfully obvious, mundane things and dealing with them in a different, which is to say better, way. Cleverness is not what's called for; perseverance is. Because you'll never be done. You must maintain that kind of vigilance day in, day out. Forevermore. That's not easy; it's also why they call it "work." Most people (one of whom wrote this sentence) tend not to find that sort of work to be attractive, and that adds to the difficulty.

So add it all up and what have we got?

"Do your job better!"

"Here's some *more* work for you to do better!"

"And while you're at it, *change* the way you're doing all that work!"

"Be sure you pay attention to all the (boring) details!"

"And get used to it, because it's never going to be done!"

Not a pretty picture. Is it any wonder that, in spite of the claims of the power and benefits of improved quality, in spite of the documented evidence to support those claims, in spite of the fact that people just flat out *know* that it's the right thing to do—improving quality is a most difficult undertaking indeed?

And that's not all. There's another significant obstacle to overcome—namely, coming to grips with the fact that:

Despite your years of training and experience in your field . . .

Despite the ferocious level of flat-out competence you have attained in your work . . .

Despite all the care you take and devotion you manifest while you're on the job . . .

Despite the buckets of sweat you expend in implementing real, systematic, intensive, committed efforts aimed at quality improvement . . .

Despite *all* these things:

A person who knows little or nothing about your business . . .

Knows little or nothing about the job you do . . .

And has put forth precisely zero effort in explicitly addressing matters of quality improvement . . .

May look at your product or service and say: "I know quality when I see it, and—naah—that ain't it."

That person is called "the customer," the person who pays

your organization money for those goods and services. And when the customer says, "That ain't it," then that, in fact, ain't it.

The truth of the matter is that *when it comes to quality, the customer has all the votes.* And knowing that, every organization needs to master "the 3 R's" of quality:

- **R**ealize that the customer has all the votes when it comes to quality.
- **R**emember that the customer has all the votes when it comes to quality.
- **R**ecognize that the fact that the customer has all the votes when it comes to quality is as it should be—that it makes perfect sense.

The other obstacles to quality—people's defensiveness, the perception of extra work, the need to change, the unglamorous nature of change—must inevitably be dealt with. But there's a fail-safe mechanism here. Even if you take no active steps to address these obstacles, they will make themselves known to you. They are part of the reality of the situation. (Or as has been said: "Reality is what happens to you while you're carrying out other plans.")

That's *not* the case with quality's 3 R's. You *can* overlook them, you *can* avoid those issues and, at least in the near term, be none the wiser. That's because as a day-in, day-out functional, operational matter you've got plenty to keep you busy—those thirty-seven things you were already doing plus the nine extras that "the quality people" want you to do. For many (most?) people in many (most?) functions in many (most?) organizations, direct impact on the customer isn't readily perceived. The customer isn't a wheel that seems to be squeaking—and besides, who's got the time to grease it, anyway?

The suggestion here is this: The fact that the customer has all the votes is the ultimate quality reality, the only one that really matters. And mastery of quality's 3 R's—by everyone in every function at *every* level in an organization—is at once an obstacle and an opportunity. Let's look at the 3 R's one at a time.

Realize that the customer has all the votes when it comes to quality.

That's simply a factual statement. The customer has the money. You want it. It's not hard to see who has the leverage in that situation. In the final analysis, your customer is going to decide what is or isn't quality and will make purchase decisions on the basis of that assessment.

Please understand that I'm not saying, "The customer decides and there is nothing you can do about it" or "The customer is going to decide anyway, so to hell with all those quality techniques!" As I've said before, the proven, powerful techniques and technologies and methodologies of quality control and quality assurance must be at the core of any serious effort to improve quality. Quality is not an abstraction; it is a measurable, manageable business issue. The problem (or, more accurately, the area under investigation) can be bounded. Measurements can and must be made. The results can and must be analyzed. The processes by which work is accomplished can and must be understood and constantly tuned and improved. And the whole cycle can and must be repeated. (Forevermore, as it happens.)

But all that bounding, measuring, analyzing, improving, and tuning does not enable an organization to (meaningfully) assert, "We have achieved quality." *Quality isn't asserted by the supplier; it's perceived by the customer.*

That notion may be disturbing to some, who may reason along these lines: "For years, businesspeople, to the extent that they paid any attention to the issue of quality, viewed it as some sort of amorphous abstraction. It was a warm, fuzzy notion that everyone could agree to but no one could do anything about. Now—finally!—people are treating it like the real, tangible business issue it is, and you're implying that they don't have control over it after all! We've made great strides in getting people to face up to their responsibility for quality, and such a notion will enable people to disavow that responsibility!"

First of all, saying that a customer can (and will) make quality judgments on the basis of "gut feel" is not the same thing as saying that you, as the supplier of goods or services, can indulge in such a nonrigorous approach. (When my first book, *I Know It When I See It,* was published, a common objection from quality professionals was: "We can't use such an abstract definition of quality as the title of your book implies." My answer was always the same: "You're right. *You* can't. But *your customers* already *are.")*

Nor is saying that, as the supplier, you don't get the ultimate vote on whether quality has been achieved the same thing as saying that you don't have effective, decisive control over quality. Consider the case of the student who is assigned a term paper. Does the student get the ultimate vote on the quality of that term paper? No. The teacher decides whether to grade the paper an A + or a C − or an F. Does the fact that the teacher gets to grade the paper imply that the student has no control over its quality? Of course not. The quality that the teacher perceives flows directly from the effort, skill, and substantive content put into that paper by the student. Does the fact that the teacher ultimately decides on the paper's grade reduce the student's responsibility one iota? I don't think so. Now, one student may say: "Hell, what's the point of spending a lot of time and effort on this project? After all, the grade will be whatever the teacher says it is!" Another student may say: "Yes, the teacher gets to decide on the grade. And the best way for me to receive the best grade possible is to plan out the project, do thorough research, and spend a lot of time and effort in creating the paper." I leave it to you to decide which student will get the better grade and whether each had effective control over the quality of the term paper.

The application of quality techniques may not enable organizations to assert, "We have achieved quality." What it does allow them to say is, "We are actively managing quality. We have formally, rigorously established our standards and efforts to improve quality. We have met those standards, and in our best judgment that gives us the highest possible likelihood that our customers will in fact assert: 'You have delivered quality.' "

In an imperfect world, that ain't half bad.

Remember that the customer has all the votes when it comes to quality.

Quality, properly dealt with, is a process-intensive issue. As a manager or supervisor, you don't (or shouldn't) spend a lot of time dealing with questions like "Is John doing his job right?" or "Why can't Mary do her job better?" For one thing, that will effectively put you into an adversarial position with John and Mary, and even if you don't know a whole lot about quality, you can probably guess that you are less likely to get improved results out of "adversaries" than out of "co-workers" or "colleagues" or "teammates." For another thing, it's been well-established that you get much further by pursuing a more process-focused line of questioning:

- What are the overall objectives of the department of which John and Mary are a part?
- Is that department meeting those objectives?
- To the extent that the department is falling short of those objectives, where do the problem areas lie?
- What is the process by which work is carried out in those areas?
- What measurements can be made to monitor the process by which work is carried out in those areas?
- How does an analysis of the results of those measurements suggest that the process can be improved?

It's in the answers to these questions (or more precisely, it's in the *process* of answering the questions) that real quality improvement can be made. But the problem (the *process* problem) is that by delving so deeply and intensively into the details of the way we work within an organization—by adopting such a hypersharpened internal focus—we can easily lose focus on the external world for which we are trying so valiantly to provide better quality.

An example. Recently I had to make a business trip that would take me from Boston to Albany, where I would catch a connecting flight to what the airlines insist on calling my "final destination" (which has always seemed like both a redundant and an unnecessarily foreboding way of putting it). Since the travel arrangements were made through a business associate's office, the plan was that I would meet him at the departure gate, and he would give me my ticket. All I had was the airline, flight number, and departure time scribbled in my pocket calendar.

Now anyone who has had to travel through Boston knows that airport access is not one of the city's more charming features. Suffice it to say that by the time I arrived at the terminal building, having squeezed my car through the Callahan Tunnel and into a too-small-by-half, approximately legal parking space in the airport parking garage, I was not as cool as a summer's breeze, either physically or temperamentally.

Things would get worse. When I arrived at the terminal building, I looked for a "departures" monitor to find out which gate my flight was leaving from. The monitor was easy to find, but the gate number wasn't. My flight wasn't listed on the screen. Fortunately, there was no line at the ticket counter.

"Can I help you, sir?" asked the ticket agent, politely and professionally.

"Yeah, I think so," I responded, frazzled and anxious. "According to my notes, I'm booked on your Flight 265 to Albany. S'posed to leave at one o'clock. But I must have gotten something wrong."

"No," he reassured me after typing a few keystrokes at his behind-the-counter computer terminal, "there's no mistake. Flight 265, Gate 26, leaving at one o'clock."

"That's good to hear. But that means you've got a problem with your departures screen."

"Really?" asked the ticket agent, genuinely concerned.

"Flight 265 isn't listed at all."

"Oh, I see what you mean," he said, relieved. "No, sir, you

don't understand. We've had such an increase in the number of flights that all our flights simply won't fit onto the monitors. So some flights just don't get listed. But there's no problem with the monitor."

"Oh, then *I see*," I said, with just the barest trace of sarcasm slipping through my otherwise perfectly professional demeanor. "In that case, you've got a problem with the sign under the monitor. It shouldn't say DEPARTURES. What it should say is A REPRESENTATIVE SAMPLING OF TODAY'S DEPARTURES."

"Sir?" he asked, still in all sincerity.

"Never mind," I said back over my shoulder. "Got a plane to catch." Whereupon I headed off to Gate 26, Albany, and my final destination.

The point is not that the ticket agent had done anything "wrong." He was fully cooperative and professional throughout our conversation. It's not that the departures monitor had malfunctioned. The ticket agent had said (and there's no reason to doubt him) that it hadn't. It's not even that the airline had made palpably wrong decisions as to how to handle the current capacity limitations of its departures monitors. Better to leave off the commuter flight carrying nine people to Albany than the 250-passenger nonstop to San Francisco. (Although it might have been helpful to have posted a small sign reading something like BECAUSE OF THE RECENT INCREASE IN THE NUMBER OF FLIGHTS, WE ARE TEMPORARILY UNABLE TO LIST ALL DEPARTING FLIGHTS ON THIS MONITOR. WE ARE IN THE PROCESS OF UPGRADING OUR SYSTEM TO ENABLE US TO LIST ALL FLIGHTS. IF YOUR FLIGHT IS NOT LISTED, PLEASE CHECK WITH ANY TICKET AGENT FOR YOUR DEPARTURE GATE AND ANY OTHER PERTINENT INFORMATION.)

The point is that in spite of—in fact, probably *because* of— a wholly sincere and admirable effort to improve and ensure the quality of service provided, the airline had managed to convince itself that there was no problem. Or rather, to the extent that a problem existed at all, it was simply that the customer "just didn't understand." And because of that, the ticket agent found himself in a debate with a customer over a quality issue. And therein lies the trap: moving from the notion that "we care a great deal about quality; we're committed to it; we're doing something about it" to the understandable but ultimately misguided assertion that "we have achieved quality."

The assertion *here* is that "the customer has all the votes when it comes to quality." If the objective is to win debates about quality ("Oh, no, sir; you're wrong—it's really not a problem"), then perhaps this assertion runs aground. If, on the other hand, the objective is to win and keep customers, then it's probably worth keeping this assertion firmly in mind.

Recognize *that the fact that the customer has all the votes when it comes to quality is as it should be—that it makes perfect sense.*

There is no getting around it: It can be very frustrating to spend so much time and effort on improving quality and then have a customer blithely say, "Nope. That ain't it." After all, you have the data, you can *prove* that the customer is wrong! ("No, sir. There's nothing wrong with the departures screen. Because of the increased number of flights etc., etc., etc.")

But when you get right down to it, it makes perfect sense. After all, isn't that precisely what it means to be a customer? In effect, by purchasing your product or service, the customer is saying: "Here's some money. I know that your job is hard. I know that a lot of skill is involved. I know that a lot of experience and expertise are involved. In fact, I know enough to know that I don't want to worry about the thousand and one details involved—all the processes involved. That's what I'm paying you to worry about." I mean, if your customers wanted to worry about all those things, they wouldn't be customers. They'd be either competitors or do-it-yourselfers (which is just another kind of competitor).

Consider. You work hard at your job. You have a nice family. You have a nice home. You'd like to be able to enjoy that nice family and nice home on weekends, so you decide to hire someone to take care of your lawn and landscaping. When you pay the bill each month, what are you paying for?

- The right not to have to worry about whether it's going to rain on Saturday afternoon, so you'd better get up early on Saturday morning to mow the lawn before it gets soaked since you won't be able to mow it again until the following weekend, by which time it will be hopelessly out of control.
- The right not to worry about whether it's really been seven years since you checked the oil in your lawn mower.
- The right to toss out the renewal notice for your subscription to *Mulch Illustrated* since you no longer really need to keep up on the latest in lawn care technology.
- The right, above all, to say—after assessing the job that the gardener has done for you: "Nope. I'm not happy with it. I'd better look for someone else." Or: "This isn't worth it. I'll just do it myself."

In short, you're paying for the right to cast the deciding vote when it comes to quality. It doesn't mean that you know more than the gardener about gardening. It doesn't mean that you're right and the gardener is wrong. But quality is not a matter of right or wrong. It's a matter of recognizing the reality of the relationship between you and your customer. (Or you and your gardener, as the case may be.) And to the extent that you deal in that reality, your chances of achieving the kind of quality results you're after will go up. By a lot.

*** *** ***

Sooner or later you have that moment of enlightenment. Whether you stumble upon it yourself or find it forced upon you, the insight is clear: "Customers make decisions on the basis of quality!"

Emphasis is usually put on the latter part of that sentence: "Customers make decisions *on the basis of quality!*" That's well and good, since it implies a need to focus on the way things are done. But once the need to formally do something about quality has been established, it's imperative to make the shift in emphasis to the front end of the sentence: "*Customers* make decisions on the basis of quality!" More specifically, the decisions customers make are purchase decisions—or as one participant in a quality seminar pointed out: "Customers are always making 'b-long-i' decisions. The question is, is it a 'buy' decision or a 'bye' decision?"

Yes, you know more about the process details of your product or service than your customers do, but that's as it should be. That's what they're paying you for. When you hold that fact up against the typical business criteria of productivity, profitability, market share, and competitive position, it's not hard to see how buy vs. bye has a somewhat more than marginal impact on an organization.

And just as this makes sense from a broad organizational perspective, so too it makes sense from a much narrower, more personal perspective. The fact of the matter is that you, as an individual, know what it is to be the customer. You know what it means to be on the receiving end of goods and services. You know what influences you. You know what you're paying for. You know what it feels like to be the customer. (And "feels like" are exactly the right words. As the customer, you're paying for the right to make judgments on the basis of feelings.)

- You know what it *feels like* to fly to Miami and have your bags sent to Milwaukee.
- You know what it *feels like* to have your new camera malfunction at the very moment your favorite nephew is being handed his diploma.
- You know what it *feels like* to be informed that you're bouncing checks all over town because of a mistake that the bank made—little consolation given the mess that you now have to clean up.

You know what those things feel like, and you also know that you don't care about all the details that an airline, a camera company, and a bank have to deal with. Not because you're not capable of understanding them or because you're not a reasonably understanding, compassionate person, but because that's precisely what you're paying *them* to worry about. That's what it means to be the customer.

The pursuit of quality does call for meeting your own, internal-to-the-organization standards, but not because those standards ought to be your ultimate goal. It's about striving to meet those internal-to-the-organization standards *because that's the best way to ensure that you'll ultimately meet your customers' standards.*

In short, improving quality is about ensuring customer satisfaction, out of which will flow significant improvements in all those important benefits for the organization as a whole as well as those for you as an individual, like job security, financial reward, career potential, and on-the-job fulfillment.

To achieve the kind of quality results every organization wants, it's essential to master the 3 R's:

1. **R**ealize that the customer has all the votes.

2. **R**emember that fact and keep it constantly in mind.

3. **R**ecognize that that's as it should be.

* * *

What this has all been about is "not losing the forest for the trees." It goes without saying that the only logical and sensible way to end such a discussion is with a (true) story about my father's Uncle Bim.

Uncle Bim ran a typical neighborhood grocery store in upstate New York in the 1930s, and my father worked for him part time. An interesting feature of Uncle Bim's operation was that he would inevitably run out of beer by the fifteenth of the month. So for the last half of every month, customers wanting beer would be told to "come back next month."

My father's curiosity eventually got the best of him. "Uncle Bim," he asked one day (presumably on the sixteenth of a month), "why don't you just order more beer so you don't run out?"

"Because," Uncle Bim responded, "I like to keep my beer bills down."

Apparently, Uncle Bim's internal-to-the-organization standard was to keep his beer bills below a certain level. That was the premise on which he operated. And given that premise, his conclusions were logical, his process was running smoothly, and quality was just fine.

The point, of course, is that Uncle Bim was missing a rather larger point. Yes, minimizing costs is an element of business success, but if you focus on it as your ultimate objective, you can wind up making some (let us be charitable) curious business decisions. And yes, establishing your own, internal-to-the-organization targets and standards is an essential part of achieving quality. But it can be terribly misguided to focus on "meeting internal standards" as the objective of your quality efforts—as the end rather than as a means to the end, with the true end being "satisfied customers."

The question of quality ultimately reduces to: Is your objective to meet your own process standards or to satisfy your customers? Those organizations that do a better job of answering it tend to be the ones that do a better job of delivering—and being rewarded for—real, relevant quality.

The Real Costs of Unquality

During a Customer Satisfaction/Quality seminar, I spent about an hour dealing with the notion that the customer has all the votes when it comes to quality. I was reasonably satisfied with the way things were going and announced a fifteen-minute coffee break. As the group dispersed, one of the participants approached me. His name was Gene, and he was the director of marketing for a company that made sophisticated electronic systems—very high-tech pieces of capital equipment carrying price tags of $1 million and up. In that kind of business, the relevant point to keep in mind is that while we tend to think in terms of the ABC Company selling a product to XYZ, Inc., there still has to be somebody at XYZ who said: "We should buy from ABC." If the ABC product performs well, that somebody is a hero. If it doesn't, well, let's just say that somebody is not such a hero. (The term "career decision" comes to mind.)

Gene said that he had an interesting story to tell me, and he was right. It was a helluva story. I asked him to repeat it to the group because it did a better job of making the connection between quality and customer satisfaction than anything we had discussed during the seminar.

Here is Gene's story.

We had just introduced a new system, and technically it was clearly the best thing going. Far more powerful, more capable, faster than anything else around.

The first installation was at a key customer's site. That's always the case in our business. We've got to begin with a solid customer of long standing, one that is willing to put up with some of the problems that inevitably arise with any new, technically advanced product.

But that doesn't mean we take those problems for granted. No, sir! We know how important quality is! So when the inevitable quality problems emerged in this case, we threw all kinds of resources at them. We put some of our local people on site to monitor the situation. We flew in some technical experts from the factory to make sure that we had the best possible resources dealing with the quality problems. We had a good handle on what the costs of these quality problems were—both to us, in terms of the expenses that go with all those resources, and to the customer, in terms of productivity lost as a result. Don't get me wrong. We weren't happy that there were any problems at all. But we were pretty satisfied about the way we were dealing with them. I thought we were being pretty enlightened, if you want to know the truth.

One day I got a call from Ed. Ed was the guy who had recommended our system for purchase, the guy who had put his faith in us. He said that he wanted to talk to me. I asked him what it was about, but he said he'd tell me when I got there. Now, this wasn't something that happened every day, but it wasn't all that unusual either. So the next day I drove over to see Ed, and I've got to admit that by the time I got there, I had just about convinced myself that the reason he wanted to see me was to thank me for what a good job we were doing dealing with the quality problems.

I knew something was off when Ed's secretary came out to meet me in the lobby and escort me back to Ed's office. He's a pretty gregarious sort who doesn't stand on a lot of ceremony—always came to meet me himself. Well, when I was ushered into his office and shook his hand, I felt like I was meeting a total stranger. He wasn't angry. He wasn't upset. He was, I don't know—beaten. He made a little small talk, but his heart definitely wasn't in it. There was an awkward silence. Then he said: "You guys croaked me." Not mad. Not angry. Just said it. We talked about it some more. I told him about all the things that we were doing to solve the quality problems. I wanted to make it clear to him that we were taking the problems very seriously and that we knew we owed it to his company to clear them up. He said that he understood and that he was appreciative, but then he repeated. "You guys croaked me." Not mad. Not angry. Hell—I wish he had yelled at me; it would have been easier to take!

Up to that point, I thought that I knew something about making measurements and analyzing the results and the costs of quality and all. But let me tell you: You really learn something about the cost of quality when you sit across the desk from somebody you've just killed professionally. We were so full of ourselves and all our clever ways of dealing with quality, thinking: "Aren't we the enlightened ones!" But it wasn't until that day that I realized what the *real* issue was. The real cost was that a customer—a living, breathing human being: somebody just like you or me, with a wife and kids and a mortgage and crabgrass—this guy had put his faith in us, and we had screwed it up, killed his career, killed his spirit.

That was painful, but it was the best quality lesson I've ever had.

The Case of the Not-So-Hot Property

[*Ben and Marcia Dalton are looking for their dream house. Married for twelve years, the Daltons have two children, ages nine and six. A third child is due in just three months. Their present house, a tidy little three-bedroom model in which they have lived for seven years, is already too cramped. And the arrival of another child is imminent. So even though they haven't been actively looking to move, they know that such a move is only a matter of time. Then they see a for-sale sign go up on a house under construction on North Street.*]

MARCIA: I almost went into labor right on the spot when I saw the sign. We've watched that house being built, and it is exactly—I mean *exactly*—the house that we've always wanted. Whenever Ben and I talk about moving, we always say: "When we move into our North Street house." That's how perfect it was for us. Well, apparently something happened with the people who were having the North Street house built—the husband got transferred out of town or something. Anyway, the house suddenly comes on the market. Just like that, a sign goes up. Like I said, I got very excited.

BEN: Excited isn't the word for it. When Marcia called me at work to tell me about it, she sounded like she was about three feet off the ground. I don't blame her. It's a great house—just the one we've been fantasizing about. So, what the hell? I mean, I know it's expensive, and I know that moving is a royal pain. And the timing could be better. After all, Marcia is due at just about the time that we'd have to move. But like they say, no guts, no glory. And besides which . . . what the hell?

[*Ben and Marcia decide to call Davisson Realty, the agency whose sign attracted them to the North Street house. Before making an offer on a new house, they want to get some information on the marketability of their present one. And since they are reasonably impressed with the people from Davisson Realty, they decide to list their house with the same agency. Alice Davisson, the owner/manager of Davisson Reality, goes out to their house and gives it a thorough inspection. After a lengthy discussion, they settle on what seems to be a reasonable list price for the house. Then they talk a bit about how long it will take to sell it. The discussions complete, the Daltons sign an exclusive listing agreement with Davisson Realty.*]

ALICE: The Daltons' home is a real little cream puff—easily the best thing on the market in that price range. My guess is that it will sell quickly—probably within four to eight weeks. Anyway, we're going to do everything we can to make sure that happens.

BEN: It's good to know that Alice thinks our house will sell so quickly. It's a pretty hairy move, making an offer on a new house and all. It could get a whole lot hairier if we wind up having trouble selling our house. Paying off two mortgages at once is not part of the plan. I have no desire to go into the real estate business.

MARCIA: We're pretty conservative people. I know that sounds crazy to say, considering how fast things have been moving, but it's true. So even though Alice says that we'll probably sell our house in under a month, we're building a little margin of safety into our offer on the new house. We're specifying a 120-day closing period. That gives us about two full months to sell our house, which Alice says should be no problem at all. That will also give me a month or so to get back on my feet after the baby comes. I can't believe we're really doing this. But it's a great house. We just can't pass it up.

[*After a couple of rounds of negotiations, the Daltons' offer on the North Street house is accepted. The 120-day closing poses no problem to the seller. A purchase-and-sale agreement is signed; things become very real and very serious. Davisson Realty goes to work marketing the Daltons' old house. There is a flurry of activity over the first two weeks of the listing, but no offers.*]

BEN: It's been hectic. The first time someone came through the house, we didn't know what to do with ourselves. We knew that we should pretty much stay out of the way. But it's a strange feeling—getting out of your house so that strangers can look through your closets. After a while you kind of get used to it. The hard part is trying to figure out whether somebody is interested or not. You say hello when people arrive, they go through your house, you say good-bye when they leave. Then you try to determine whether they're going to make a thirty-year commitment involving hundreds of thousands of dollars. It's nuts.

MARCIA: It's beginning to get on my nerves. We've probably had eight or ten different groups of people go through our house in the past two weeks, but nobody from Davisson ever called us to give us any feedback. I finally called Alice to complain. She told me that as soon as somebody showed some interest, she'd get back to us. If there is no interest, she won't make a follow-up call. She said she didn't want to bother us unnecessarily. I don't know, though. I think I'm more bothered by not hearing anything than I would be by a simple phone call. At least that way we wouldn't be left wondering. I'll really be glad when this is over.

ALICE: The Daltons are just going through some basic "seller anxiety." We see it all the time. Marcia called me. She was concerned that they hadn't been getting any follow-up phone calls after we had a showing. What she didn't understand was that it's our standard operating procedure to follow up only if interest is shown. That way we don't bother the seller unless we have to. And by not having to make those phone calls, we have more time to devote to selling. It works out better for everybody. And right now that extra selling time could come in handy—the market seems to have turned a little softer. I wish we knew why, but I guess that's life in the house-selling business.

[Alice's observation about the market softening turns out to be an accurate one. Over the next two months, sales activity at the Daltons' house slows down considerably, with an average of about one and a half showings per week.]

MARCIA: This is beginning to get on my nerves. At least with a baby, you have a pretty good idea as to when "the big event" will occur. But selling a house— Things have really slowed down. I can't say that I miss the fire drills we were having when the house first went on the market. You know: we'd get a phone call that someone would be over to see the house in twenty minutes. You ever try to pick up a seven-room house in twenty minutes? With two kids? But at least then we were given twenty minutes' notice. Last week, a guy named Larry from Davisson shows up at the door unannounced. No phone call. With a couple and a bunch of kids and somebody I assume is the kids' grandfather. They want to go through the house. Here I am, eight months pregnant, chasing two kids around the house, and the doorbell rings and I've got "The Waltons" on my front step and I'm supposed to let them go through my house. They went through the house all right, but it was "as is." It looked like a direct hit. I can't say I'm surprised that they weren't interested. At that moment I didn't like my house a whole lot either. But Davisson should have called. I don't know—I'm beginning to wonder about them a whole lot.

BEN: In two weeks, we'll have three children. A month after that, we'll have two mortgages. I'm not an accountant, but I think our finances are a bit on the rocky side. At this point I wish we had been turned down for the mortgage on the North Street house. That's what we get for having good credit. Things are getting kind of tense. I've never seen Marcia so upset as she was the day that the Davisson guy showed up with a cast of thousands. What Marcia doesn't know, because I didn't tell her, is that I got a call from Alice the other day. She wants to run an open house on Sunday, the eighth. Marcia's due date is the third. So Alice expects us to worry about having the house in shape for an open house just when Marcia will be coming home from the hospital with a new baby. I told Alice that I didn't think it was a very good idea. Unbelievable.

ALICE: I know that this isn't the right way to think, but I'm getting a bit tired of dealing with the Daltons' complaints. The market has slowed down to nothing. We've got fifty-one listings in this office alone; that's an all-time high. None of the properties are moving. And the Daltons are acting like theirs is the only house we're handling. And we're busting our tails for them. Hell, they're scheduled to close on their North Street property in about six weeks. That's *our* listing. You think we want anything to happen to keep that sale from going through? They may not realize it, but they've been getting special service and attention from us. Just last week we had what looked like a good prospect referred to us by Callahan Realty. It turned out that these people were looking for a house exactly like the Daltons' house, in a neighborhood exactly like the Daltons' neighborhood. We called to set up an appointment, but there was no answer. Now, these people were serious buyers. They were ready to make an offer on another house, but Callahan's convinced them to look at one more house— the Daltons' house. They had all their kids with them and one of the grandfathers who apparently was going to finance the purchase. That meant that there would be no banks to muddy things up. A quick closing. So I told Larry to go over even though we didn't have an appointment; we didn't want to lose the prospect. Well, Larry goes over and the showing is a disaster. Larry says things were so messed up it looked like the Daltons had just held a rodeo inside the house. And apparently Marcia was rude to Larry and didn't exactly make the customers feel welcome. Honestly, I don't know sometimes. To top it all off, a couple of days later I call the Daltons to talk about setting up an open house, and Ben tells me that the date is less than a week after Maria is due and he doesn't think it's such a good idea. Well, they've got to decide how serious they are about selling their house.

[*Two weeks later, Marcia has a baby girl. 7 pounds, 5 ounces, 21 inches, wonderfully healthy. One month after that, Alice calls the Daltons with the news that she has a very interested buyer in hand, and she's sure that an offer will be made "either today or tomorrow." The Daltons are thrilled. They are also very busy, since they closed on their North Street house the day before, and are moving in, as luck would have it, today and tomorrow. Marcia points out to Ben that the timing is actually pretty good: "The move will take our minds off the offer on the other house." Ben agrees. Two days later, after moving into their new home, they still haven't heard from Alice Davisson about the prospective buyer. They call her. It is the first phone call they have made from the North Street house.*]

BEN: I call and Alice tells me that something happened and her hot prospect turned out not to be so hot after all. I said that those things happen, but why didn't she let us know? She said she would have, but we didn't have a phone. Can you imagine that? I mean, it isn't as though she doesn't know where we've moved to. She sold us the damn house! It's two miles from her office. It was reasonable to assume that we would be home. If she had driven by, the seventy-five-foot moving van parked out front might have given her a hint.

MARCIA: First Davisson sells us a bill of goods about how fast and easy it will be to sell our house. Then things drag on for months. All the while we're getting lousy service. Then, in the middle of a move, Alice gets our hopes up. And she knows a day in advance that we aren't going to get an offer and she doesn't tell us? She put us through another sleepless night. I mean, we've got all the sleepless nights we want with the new baby. We don't need any help in that department. I want to fire Davisson right now. Ben says that at this point it would be cutting off our nose to spite our face. He says he's been asking around, and it seems that all real estate agencies are like that. So there's no guarantee that it will be any better with anyone else. "The devil you know" and all. I know he's right, but it sure would feel good to keep Davisson from getting the commission. Five percent! For what?!?

ALICE: I've gotta get out of this business. Now the Daltons are upset because I didn't get into my car and drive over to tell them that there was nothing to tell them! Maybe they'd like me to cook dinner for them while I'm there. Maybe change the baby's diapers. We've spent I don't know how much in advertising and showings and everything else that goes with it, and we have nothing to show for it. On top of that, I have to listen to their complaints every day? No, thank you. You'd think they were the first people who ever wound up with two mortgages. Hell, right now I've got sixty-two houses that I can't sell! Do I call the Daltons to complain about that? Don't get me wrong—I know they're under a lot of pressure. And I don't talk to them this way. I'm always perfectly cordial and professional. But I didn't get into this business in order to wet-nurse a pair of obsessive-compulsives who think that they're the only ones with problems. That's for sure. It's just not worth the aggravation.

[*A month later, the Daltons get an offer on their house. It's about 10 percent below their asking price (and about 5 percent below what they can really afford to settle for) but they decide to take the offer. Seven weeks later, they pass papers on the house. Alice is present at the closing and is given her commission check by the bank attorney. Things are cordial but strained. She wishes Ben and Marcia good luck in their new house. They thank her and wish her well. Their house now sold, the Daltons leave the bank.*]

BEN: Well, I've sure learned a lot. About myself. About the real estate business. Boy, did I learn a lot about the real estate business! I wish it was a business I had some interest in, because I think I could do it better than most of the people who are in real estate. You see, I've just been through it. I know what it's like to be on the other side. I know what people want from a realtor. They're paying a lot of money for that service, and I don't think that they're getting it.

MARCIA: We made a lot of mistakes over this whole process of trying to sell our house. And we've learned a lot from those mistakes. The trouble is that we probably won't ever get a chance to do anything with the lessons that we've learned because we don't plan to move again. Ever! I suppose our experience could come in handy in advising our kids when the time comes for them to buy a house, but let's be serious: Nobody listens to parents about those sorts of things. I thought a lot over the last seven months about what it would feel like to finally sell our house. I thought I would be very sad and emotional. It was the first house we ever owned—the house we raised our kids in. It was a good house to us. And I thought I'd be excited. But you know, I don't feel any of those things. I just feel numb. I just feel like, you know, "I'm glad that's finally over with." Like it was a final exam or a trip to the dentist or something. And that bothers me—because it shouldn't feel like that. It should be a very happy, exciting moment, and it isn't. I feel like that excitement is something that Davisson Realty stole from me, and I'll never forget that.

QUIZ
The Case of the Not-So-Hot-Property

1. Alice Davisson made such an impression on the Daltons that they named their new baby daughter after her. What is the baby's name?
   a. Alice Dalton.
   b. Davisson Dalton.
   c. Cream Puff Dalton.
   d. Because-of-you-we-went-through-seven-months-of-emotional-torture-so-now-we-hope-your-business-goes-under Dalton.

2. If someone were to call the Daltons asking for their advice about selling a house, what would their response most likely be?
   a. Don't do it.
   b. Do it, but don't use a real estate broker; sell it yourself.
   c. Do it, but don't use Davisson Realty.
   d. Do it, and if you decide to use Davisson Realty, jerk 'em around a little for us.

3. Fundamentally, what were the Daltons buying from Davisson Realty?
   a. A bad case of heartburn.
   b. The privilege of having total strangers make rude remarks about their taste in decorating.

   c. A house-selling service.

   d. A hand-holding-throughout-the-whole-anxiety-pro-voking-emotion-laden-checkbook-pinching-process-of-trying-to-sell-a-house service.

4. From Alice Davisson's point of view, did her agency deliver quality service to the Daltons?

   a. Yes, because she eventually sold their house.

   b. Yes, because all the words were spelled right and the grammar was correct on the purchase-and-sale agreement.

   c. Yes, because the agency rigorously followed its standard operating procedure.

   d. Yes, because she was always "perfectly cordial and professional" even though she felt the Daltons were "a pair of obsessive-compulsives" who thought they were the only ones with problems.

5. From the Daltons' point of view, did Davisson Realty provide quality service?

   a. No, because they had to settle for a much lower price than they had hoped for.

   b. No, because it took them a lot longer to sell their house than Davisson Realty had led them to think it would.

   c. No, because of problems like the poor phone follow-up, the no-notice showings, the thoughtless scheduling of an open house, and the hot prospect that wasn't.

   d. No, because they felt they had been put through seven months of emotional torture and were reminded of that fact every time they called their baby daughter by name.

6. Who was right?

   a. Alice Davisson, because she's the pro; she understands the real estate business a lot better than people like the Daltons.

   b. The Daltons, because they were the customers and "the customer is always right."

    c. Larry, because the house *did* look like a rodeo had been held in it.

    d. No one. It's not a matter of right or wrong; it's a matter of "Who is paying money to whom for what?"

7. Who won?

    a. Davisson Realty, because when all was said and done, the agency did collect a 5 percent commission.

    b. The Daltons, because when all was said and done, they did sell their house.

    c. Grandpa Walton, because the first time his daughter and son-in-law missed a mortgage payment on the house they eventually bought, he foreclosed and sold it back to them at a huge profit.

    d. No one, because once the supplier of goods or services puts itself into a contentious position with its customers, the game is lost.

"I Guess You're Right—Good-Bye"

"There's something amiss with the clock's second hand.
It goes counterclockwise; I don't understand."
"But you see—we're the experts. That's how it was planned."
"I guess you're right. Good-bye."

"I think that this fridge's quality's poor.
The light should go on when you open the door!"
"Nope—not according to spec zero-point-four."
"I guess you're right. Good-bye."

"You billed me for shipments, but my records don't list them.
I don't want to pay you; I couldn't have missed them!"
"I hear what you say, but the system's the system."
"I guess you're right. Good-bye."

"She decides on my credit with no one to offer her
The advice and assistance that clearly are called for here?"
"Then why else would we call her 'a loan' officer?"
"I guess you're right. Good-bye."

"The busiest flight of the day, you might note,
I don't think should depart from a gate so remote."
"But what makes you think that you get a vote?"
"I guess you're right. Good-bye."

" 'Good-bye' is what they said—the fools!
They may make sense, but we make the rules!"

Moral
Except for the number-one rule from the hard knocks schools:
"I guess good-bye is right."

3

What Is Quality?

It has been said: "Quality is that higher-order thing that makes the rest of life worth living." (Or at least it has *now* been said.) Another notion: "Quality is the stuff of inherent worthwhileness, intrinsic virtue, superiority in kind." Still another: "Quality is so sublime as to foil our efforts to capture its essence with mere thoughts and words. It is a butterfly for which there is no net."

When I hear definitions like these, I think, "How poetic." That's usually followed by something more along the lines of, "What a load of crap!"

It's important not to be afraid to make such bold assertions, because (1) it is a load of crap and (2) everybody knows that it's a load of crap. Everybody knows that the reason such lofty, high-falutin' definitions of quality are so common is that they enable people to avoid having to *do* much of anything about quality. After all, if quality is this transcendent thing, something too important to be lumped in with all our petty day-to-day concerns, then much as we'd like to, we can't really *do* much of anything about it, now can we, so let's get on with business as usual. A colleague once described such lofty characterizations as "pillow definitions": They're soft, they feel good to cuddle up against, and they can help you sleep your way through the moment at hand. It is heartening to note that more and more organizations are abandoning their pillow definitions of quality. It would be even more heartening if this development were the result of cool analysis and dispassionate reflection. In reality, it is usually the result of an impassioned reaction to circumstances that are finally recognized as being dangerous, bordering on fatal—but, as the saying goes, we'll take it any way we can get it.

People tend to get religion about quality following a moment of reckoning. The best "moment of reckoning" story I ever heard comes from the electronics industry. It occurred in the early 1980s, at a time when U.S. electronics companies were being severely beaten up in the marketplace and in the press over the quality of their products relative to the quality of their Japanese competitors' products.

As the story is told, one very large U.S. electronics company found itself with a need to order a number of small electrical components—let's say, 10,000 capacitors. So a bunch of clever managers said to themselves: "OK. These Japanese companies are supposed to be such hotshot makers of quality products. Let's give them a chance to prove that they're really as good as everybody says they are."

So they placed an order for the 10,000 capacitors with one of the Japanese hotshots, but as a condition of the order they stipulated what was by typical American standards of the day an unheard-of quality criterion. In the order they said, "We will accept *three* bad components in the entire lot of 10,000." Pretty tough stuff. You can almost see them sending off the order with a sort of stick-that-in-your-pipe-and-smoke-it swagger.

Severals weeks later, on the exact date shipment was promised (which is no small feat (and no trivial point)), the order of capacitors arrived. When the box was opened, a note was found along with the capacitors. It began:

Thank you very much for your order. We are honored to have been given the opportunity to serve you.

Sure, sure. So far so good. But then the note went on:

We were confused about one aspect of your order, though. We couldn't understand why you would *want* three defective components.

It got better still.

But we made them, and we packed them separately on the assumption that you would not want them to get mixed in with the rest, thereby polluting your manufacturing operation.

Sure enough, there in the box was a separate little envelope containing three capacitors, each one specially made to be defective and clearly labeled as such.

Now, you don't have to be a quality expert to recognize that there is a nontrivial difference between an approach that sees quality as "a butterfly" and one that sees a single bad capacitor as "polluting" a manufacturing operation. It doesn't really matter whether the story is apocryphal or not. The fact that such a story could be widely told is evidence that people have begun to recognize the difference. It is when that difference makes itself known with the ever so subtle jolt of a ball-peen hammer to the forehead that "a moment of reckoning" occurs.

And that's good. People begin to realize that quality isn't just an apple-pie-and-motherhood matter. They begin to realize that quality is a serious business issue that can and must be dealt with like other serious business issues. They discard their feels-good definitions of quality and begin to approach things in a much more rigorous, analytical, precise, and hard-edged way.

All this activity usually begins with the adoption of one of the "standard" definitions of quality. The standard definition of quality to which I subscribe is this: Quality means "conformance to requirements." You must clearly and explicitly define the requirements: "Part 24-D shall be 1.50cm long (+/− 0.01cm) by 0.76cm wide (+/− 0.01cm)." "Each teller shall handle 120 transactions per eight-hour shift." "A direct mail marketing campaign must achieve an active reply rate of 1.5 percent." And so on. You must then compare the actual results achieved against the clearly defined requirements. If they match—if there is conformance to requirements—you have achieved quality. If they don't, you haven't. Period.

The acceptance of such a hard-edged view of quality by an organization (or an individual within an organization) is truly a watershed moment. It forces the organization to confront reality by establishing targets and *doing the things necessary to hit those targets.* (Nobody said it would be easy.) "If you don't know where you're going, any road'll get you there," as the saying goes. Clearly and explicitly defined requirements are the statement of that destination. Insisting on and doing the things necessary to ensure conformance are the steps along the journey. It can be a long and difficult journey. That's why an emphasis on setting internal specifications is so essential to the achievement of quality. Otherwise, to coin another phrase, you can't get there from here.

The clear statement of and adherence to internal, operational specifications, in all functions and departments throughout an organization, are absolutely necessary to quality improvement.

Necessary, but not sufficient. Suppose you go into a stationery store to purchase a ball point pen. The clerk behind the counter says to you: "How about this pen? It looks great. It feels great. It writes very smoothly. And it will work without a refill for six full months." So you buy the pen, and you take it home, and it does look great and feel great and write great. But it runs out of ink in four months, not in six months.

QUESTION: As the customer, how do you feel about the quality of that pen?

ANSWER: Probably not very good.

Now let's go back in time: same store, same clerk, same

pen. This time the clerk says to you: "Buy this pen. It looks great, writes great, feels great—and it will write without a refill for *three* full months." You buy it. It looks, writes, and feels great. Three months come and go—and it's still writing! It writes for four full months!

QUESTION: Now how do you feel about the quality of that pen?

ANSWER: Probably a whole lot better.

But why? It was the same pen, the same measurable performance, the same length of time before the ink ran out. The only difference in the two cases was your *expectation* of what the pen would do. When you expected six months but got four months, you translated that into—you perceived that as— lousy quality. When you expected three months but got four months, you perceived that to be perfectly acceptable quality, maybe even exceptional quality.

"Expectations" is an important notion, and it begins to suggest that there is more to this business of quality than properties inherent in the product itself, like its length or its weight or its color.

Consider what it was like when you bought a new car in the early 1970s. Naturally, in the first few days after you drove the car home from the dealer you were very sensitive to how the car was performing. You tended to notice things. Like a slight rattle or vibration when you hit a certain speed. Or a piece of trim that was a little bit loose. Or a strange odor coming from somewhere below the driver's seat. So you made up a list and you brought the car in for service to clear up those little bugs (along with, perhaps, three or four other minor problems). And the dealer took good care of you; it was all under warranty. Obliging mechanics tightened up a bolt and that took care of the rattle. They glued the piece of loose trim back into place. They removed the half-eaten baloney sandwich that had been left in the car's left rocker panel, and that (eventually) cleared up the odor. You might have had to repeat this little routine once or twice during the first few months you owned the car, but eventually all the little bugs were shaken out.

When that happened to you, say, fifteen years ago, how did you feel about the quality of your car? Probably not so bad. "After all," a reasonable person would have concluded, "a car is a big, complex thing to have to build. You have to *expect* a few things to go wrong."

But do you? After all, if you purchased exactly the same car today with exactly the same number of "little things" gone wrong, and if you had to make exactly the same number of trips in for service and received exactly the same level of service as you had in the early 1970s—how would you feel about the quality of that car now? How understanding would you be? How accepting would you be?

In all likelihood, not very. But what changed? Did the car change? No, it was exactly the same. Have you become any less reasonable? No. But you probably have become more demanding. Your expectations for a new car have changed, and with them the level of quality that you perceive in a given car has changed as well.

Quality *is* conformance to requirements, but merely stating that definition begs an important question: *What are the requirements to which a supplier of goods or services must conform?*

We have already discussed one critical set of requirements: the *specifications* established within the organization. I would like to suggest that there is another, equally critical set of requirements: the *expectations that customers have* for the goods and services that the organization provides. Unless there is conformance to *both* sets of requirements—specifications and expectations alike—quality hasn't been achieved.

Let's slice this notion of expectations a bit finer by considering two types of expectations: macro- and microexpectations.

Macroexpectations are the larger, more global expectations that a customer brings to any business dealings. They can be (roughly) equated with "standard industry practice of the day."

The car example above illustrates dealing with macroexpectations. Over the past fifteen years, the marketplace's overall sense of "what it means to buy a car" has changed. If you want to sell cars to people but offer a product that doesn't conform to their changed expectations, you are unlikely to succeed, and the reason will be quality. If you doubt that, apply this test: You buy a new car from a dealer, perceive some quality problems, and take the car in to the dealer to register a complaint. In response to your complaint, the dealer pulls out a yellowing, dog-eared piece of paper, blows the dust off of it, hands it to you, and says, "Ah, but you don't understand. We haven't changed our specifications since 1972, and we're still hitting those specs dead on, so you're wrong when you say we have quality problems." Would you consider the dealer to have addressed your complaint? Would you now feel better about the quality of your car, knowing that it was performing according to the specifications written down on a piece of paper in the dealer's desk? He might have hit his specifications. But he didn't hit your expectations. *Therefore,* he didn't deliver quality.

If your objective is to win debates with your customers over who knows more about your products and services, then yes, by all means get into a battle of "specs-manship." If, on the other hand, your objective is to win and keep customers, then factoring in customer expectations is the only effective approach. I'm not challenging the "conformance to requirements" definition of quality. I'm merely extending the definition of relevant requirements to include that important set of customer expectations.

Microexpectations are the much smaller, much more focused expectations that customers have when doing business with you. Unlike with macroexpectations, which tend to move glacially and as a result of the activities of all the players in an industry, you *do* have direct and immediate control over microexpectations.

The pen example above calls attention to the importance of microexpectations. When the clerk said the pen would last six months, its quality, as perceived by the customer, became unacceptable. When the clerk said three months, the quality suddenly got a whole lot better. The connection is that direct and causal. It behooves you, therefore, to devote a high degree of effort and attention to the care and feeding of micro-expectations.

"But," goes the counterargument, "the clerk didn't make the product. The pen company did. Its specification may well have been three months all along, and almost certainly never was six months." And that's probably true. But it's also spectacularly uninteresting to the customer. Remember: Keeping straight all the details of the designing, manufacturing, and distribution of pens is precisely what the customer is paying someone else to worry about.

All of which leads to two key points:

1. Perceived quality—quality as it is *felt* by the customer—is a function of *expectations.*
2. In the final analysis, perceived quality is the only quality that matters, since what the customer perceives *is* what the customer receives.

Quality is not what happens when what you do matches your intentions. It's what happens when what you do matches your customers' expectations. When you strip away all the complexity and distractions of your business (which is another way of saying "when you look at things from your customers' perspective"), the quest for quality comes down to the answer to a very basic customer question: "Did you or didn't you give me what I paid you to give me?" If you can answer yes, then you've achieved quality. If you can't, then you haven't. (And if you are going to hold on to the notion that you, not your customers, get to decide what quality is, you can take solace in the notion that pretty soon you won't have many customers with opinions on the matter to cause you such inconvenience.)

This points directly to a most useful refinement of the standard definition of quality:

Quality is that which meets the customer's expectations.

Why that refinement? Two reasons. First, as discussed in Chapter 2, in the hustle and bustle of organizational life, it can be easy to get so caught up in internal organizational matters that you lose sight of the fact that it's ultimately the customer who gets all the votes. Your own internal/operational requirements and specifications are such internal matters. Absolutely essential internal matters, and ferociously important internal matters, but internal matters nonetheless. And to the extent that you are sincerely committed to quality—that you really want to *do something* about quality—a focus on specifications can insulate you from that reality. Second, unless you have explicit reminders, it can be easy to forget that customer expectations exist, and if you forget that they exist, then the odds of meeting them will tend to go down rather significantly.

The simple Venn diagram shown above suggests that quality (**Q**) is what occurs in the area of overlap of the three circles: specifications (**S**), macroexpectations (**E**), and microexpectations (**e**). In a perfect world, those three circles would be fully congruent. Your specifications would map onto your customers' macroexpectations *exactly,* and both would map onto those customers' microexpectations *exactly.* In the real world, though, that tends not to happen. There is usually some degree of nonconformance, shown in the diagram as the (tinted) areas where the three circles do not overlap. (Analogies to friction loss and entropy come to mind, but somehow I don't think that a digression into Quality and the Second Law of Thermodynamics is the sort of thing that "the rest of us" are interested in.) Achieving quality can therefore be thought of as an effort to keep the three circles overlapped to the greatest degree possible.

If you prefer a verbal (as opposed to diagrammatic) mnemonic, try this:

Specifications + macroexpectations + microexpectations = quality
Which suggests:
$$S + E + e = Q$$
Which suggests the word **SEeQ** (as in "hide and go . . ."), which in turn suggests the question:

How do I find this elusive thing called quality?
The answer to which is:

SEeQ and ye shall find.

Let's look at how this **SEeQ** approach to quality might be applied.

✳ ✳ ✳

The "airport departures screen" story in Chapter 2 is an example of a quality problem arising out of nonconformance to a macroexpectation. Because of the increase in the number of flights offered, the airline could not fit all departing flights onto the departures monitors in the airport. Some decisions had to be made about which ones to list and which ones to leave off, and the monitors accurately reflected the decisions that had been made. Thus, the airline had achieved conformance to its own specifications.

As a passenger, however, I had every reason to think that my flight would be listed on the departures monitor. That's a macroexpectation that passengers—in all airports, with all airlines—have come to have. So when the flight wasn't listed, the stage was set for the quality problem that occurred.

Conformance to specifications? Yes.

Conformance to expectations? No.

Quality? No.

✳ ✳ ✳

The story of the Daltons' dream house in Chapter 2 illustrates quality problems caused by microexpectations, i.e., expectations over which Davisson Realty had very direct and very immediate control. It was "standard operating procedure" for Davisson Realty to follow up with a client after a showing only if the prospect expressed interest in buying the house. But it was clear that the Daltons expected follow-up phone calls after all showings. So when the calls didn't come, the Daltons became dissatisfied with the quality of the service they were receiving. Davisson Realty had conformed to its own specifications (i.e., standard operating procedures) but not to its customers' expectations. Quality problems resulted, and the business relationship began to disintegrate quickly.

How do you find out what customers' expectations are? Simple. You ask, the theory being that your chances of finding something increase dramatically as you spend more time looking. And you ask customers as directly as possible, the theory being that you should spend your time looking in the places where that something is most likely to be.

✳ ✳ ✳

You purchase a new color television set, bring it home, plug it in, and turn it on—only to discover that the picture is terrible, the color anything but lifelike. You call the store and register a complaint about the quality of your new TV set. (Clearly, it has not met your expectations.) A serviceman arrives a couple of hours later to check things out. "First I have to do a few things to tune the set in. Then I have to de-gauss it for you. Then you should be in business," the serviceman says. Whereupon he fiddles with a variety of meters and gauges, pokes at various knobs and components in the back of the TV set, all the while bending like a contortionist in order to see the image of the TV picture in the mirror that he has propped up on the floor in front of the set. When he finishes with those procedures, he takes out a small wire hoop, plugs it in, and waves it in abracadabra circles in front of the picture tube. And believe it or not, as a result of all those machinations, the picture gets demonstrably better.

QUESTION: Has the quality problem been solved?

ANSWER: It depends.

More specifically, it depends on exactly when this little scenario took place. Suppose the time was 1957, back in the earliest days of color television. In those days, the picture tube was rounded at the corners, the cabinet was as big as a moderate-size meat locker (but didn't feel much like a meat locker since early TV sets threw off enough heat to trip the average sprinkler system), and about the only programs broadcast in color were "Bonanza" and the World Series, but it was, by God, color! (Or as it was said at the time, *living* color!) Thirty years ago, color TVs did have to be "tuned in" when they were "installed," and they also had to be de-gaussed from time to time. (That's what the wire hoop and abracadabra business was all about. Something to do with breaking up the magnetic field that would build up around the picture tube. At least that's how I remember it being explained to me, which will have to do for now.)

Now, at the moment that you, as the customer, perceived a quality problem, a quality problem existed. But thirty years ago, it could have been pretty easily rectified. When the serviceman checked out the set, he would first determine whether the specifications component of quality was OK—that is, whether the set was performing as it was designed to perform. Let's suppose that the specs checked out OK. There would still be a problem with expectations—in this case, microexpectations. No one ever told you the set had to be tuned in or de-gaussed. So when the set didn't work very well, you assumed that there was a quality problem. And there was. Once your expectation was adjusted ("That's the way all our sets work before they're tuned in and de-gaussed"), the quality problem was cleared up.

How could the problem have been avoided in the first place? Any number of ways. Salespeople could have informed you of the need for "installation service" when you bought the set. A card could have been taped to the screen, containing that same information. As for preventing future quality problems, the serviceman could inform you that you should call to arrange a de-gaussing every six months or so. Your expectations would now be properly set, so when the picture's color resolution started to deteriorate in six months, you wouldn't think: "What's wrong with this set?!?" You would think, instead, "It's time to get the set de-gaussed."

The point is that:

- Hitting your customers' expectations is a quality requirement.
- The process can be tuned to ensure that there is conformance to that requirement.

Suppose now that this scenario were taking place today rather than in 1957. You certainly would still perceive a quality problem, but when the serviceman came and went through his tuning and de-gaussing routine, explaining that this was perfectly standard, perfectly normal ("That's the way all our sets work before they're tuned in and de-gaussed"), would the quality problems be cleared up? Probably not. Why not? Because of the change in the *macroexpectations* of the marketplace over the past thirty years. What do you expect when you buy a color television set today? Like everyone else, you expect to bring it home, plug it in, and have it work without any service or maintenance for nine or ten years. Even after the serviceman's visit, the quality problem would still exist because there would still be nonconformance with your expectations for "what a color TV ought to be like." (Hell, the nonconformance would be greater than ever. I don't know about you, but if someone came into my living room and waved a wire hoop in front of my TV, it wouldn't make *me* feel better.) The resolution of this problem is not a simple matter of explaining to the customer that tuning and degaussing are normal. The resolution here is redesigning the product to ensure conformance with macroexpectations.

❋ ❋ ❋

Remember what it used to be like on payday? You'd get your paycheck and hustle down to the bank to cash it, hoping to arrive before the other 750 people you worked with—who also got paid that day. Otherwise, you'd have to spend your entire lunch hour standing in line.

Then along came something called "direct deposit," and you never really got a check any more, just a receipt indicating that your pay for that period had been deposited to your account. So now you could enjoy a nice, leisurely lunch in the company cafeteria without getting heartburn (or at least without getting heartburn as a result of having rushed to the bank).

Today, you've come a lot further still. Not only don't you have to go to the bank during your lunch hour. You don't have to go to the bank at all for routine transactions, like making deposits and withdrawals and checking to see how much you don't have in your balance. Now you can do all that stuff at 2:30 in the morning in a supermarket parking lot because now there are Automatic Teller Machines, or ATMs. These are a tremendous convenience—until the day that you pull up to your ATM (the one that's just half a mile from your house) and discover that it is "down" and won't be back "up" for ten minutes. Ten minutes!

Now you have a choice. You can wait the ten minutes, but that's an unacceptable waste of time. (Never mind that you used to spend thirty minutes staring at the back of the bad raincoat in front of you in line every payday, so the odd ten minutes here and there aren't going to kill you.) Or you can drive over to the next closest ATM, but that's a mile and a half away. (Never mind that that's still three miles closer than the nearest branch bank you used to have to go to—besides which it's unlikely that that branch would have been open at 2:30 in the morning, anyway.) No, instead you decide to do the sensible thing. You decide to get very upset about the quality of service you've been receiving—after all, this is the third time it's happened in the past six months!—and you go back home to write an angry letter to the bank registering your complaint.

QUESTION: Is there a quality problem?

ANSWER: If you, the customer, perceive a quality problem, then there is a quality problem.

What is the source of the problem? After receiving your letter, the bank would (and probably should) first look at the specifications component of quality. What uptime requirement has been defined for ATMs? Does that particular ATM conform to that requirement? If not, why not? What can be done about it?

Naturally, if it turns out the ATM's history of failure is outside the process "control limits" (sorry: a bit of technical talk), then corrective steps should be taken. But suppose that ATM does conform to the uptime requirement. There is still the matter of nonconformance to a macroexpectation to be dealt with.

Consider how your expectations for "what it means to do my banking" have changed over the years. A decade ago, you might have spent several minutes, several times each week standing in line in banks. That is the way it was, what you expected. But that's not the way it is any more. Now you're conditioned to driving half a mile, running in, running out—at whatever time suits you best—and your banking is done. Your expectation is that banking is "invisible" to you and you're perfectly happy to keep it that way.

The bank could try to get into a game of specs-manship and "prove" to you that even with the three "ATM down" situations in the last six months you have still saved a total of x minutes (hours?) as a result of the service and convenience provided you by the network of teller machines. But from your perspective, a ten-minute delay can be significant. It doesn't *feel* like "just ten minutes." It feels like "a 100 percent increase in the time devoted to banking."

The point is that a gap exists between what you got and what you expected, you perceived that gap as a quality gap, and *therefore* it was a quality gap. And to the extent that other customers are perceiving the same nonconformance to expectations, the bank has a serious quality problem.

How can the bank deal with the problem? It can change its internal specifications for ATM uptime and make the necessary design changes to increase reliability for the machines. It can put a second ATM at the site in question. Or it can take steps to ensure that customers' expectations conform more closely to the availability of the ATMs—for example, by posting the schedule for routine maintenance on the door of each ATM so customers know that the system is more likely to be down on a given day, at a given time.

The concern here is not so much the specific steps that can be taken to deal with a quality problem. The point is that a quality problem is more likely to be identified if the situation is viewed from the customer's perspective. Quality problems arising from "broken expectations" (i.e., nonconformance to customer expectations) must first be identified before they can be dealt with effectively.

✳ ✳ ✳

A friend calls to tell you that she'll pick you up at 7:30. It's going to be tight, but you rush home, bolt down your dinner, shower, change your clothes, and sit waiting by the door at 7:25. Your friend shows up at 8:15. You are not pleased.

QUESTION: Had she said 8:15 in the first place, thereby more carefully setting the proper microexpectation, would the "unquality" in this situation have been avoided?

ANSWER: Quite possibly.

QUESTION: Once your friend realized that she was running late, might a phone call to apprise you of that fact, thereby resetting the relevant microexpectation, have helped to minimize the unquality in this situation?

ANSWER: Very likely.

QUESTION: Does your friend's track record for punctuality, which in effect has established a macroexpectation with you, have anything to do with your overall perception of the situation and willingness to make allowances?

ANSWER: Most definitely. If this was an aberration, and she explained to you the complicated circumstances that had led to her being late, you'd be more likely to forgive her. If, on the other hand, this was just another chapter in a continuing saga . . .

* * *

To sum up the logic behind all these examples:

- The reality is that customer expectations exist, whether or not you choose to do anything about them.
- Customers perceive quality relative to those expectations.
- Perceived quality is, in the final analysis, the only relevant measure of quality.
- Under the circumstances, it is important to actively monitor, measure, and manage expectations.

The **SEeQ** model can be a valuable diagnostic tool. Using it as a guide, you can more effectively (1) understand what your customers' expectations are; (2) set and, when necessary, reset those expectations; and (3) reconcile your internal/operational specifications with those expectations. As a result, you will be far more likely to have a handle on the true nature of the quality situation that you face. That, in turn, means that you will be far more likely to deal with it successfully.

✳ ✳ ✳

This whole book is about the importance of viewing things from the customer's perspective. If you are reading this, you are my customer. So let me take a few moments to address some issues that might have occurred to you.

Does all this emphasis on expectations mean that we don't have to conform to our own, internal/operational requirements?

No, no, no. I began by saying that "quality is conformance to requirements." I then said that definition could be refined to "quality is that which meets the customer's expectations." I can make a further refinement to that definition and say that "quality means doing whatever it takes to meet the customer's expectations." And the most important "whatever it takes" is to have a good handle on the specifications component of quality. Without well-defined and vigilantly pursued internal/operational requirements and specifications, the odds of ultimately meeting customers' expectations will not just go down rather significantly; they will fall to approximately zero. The question is: Toward what end have those internal/operational requirements and specifications been defined? This "customer expectation" definition of quality will help keep them focused where they belong: on the external realities of the marketplace.

Years ago, quality was this thing that we didn't think we had much control over. By focusing on our internal/operational requirements, we've gained a strong sense of control. Won't this emphasis on customer expectations cause us to relinquish a lot of that control?

Only if you assume that you have no control over your customers' expectations. Consider the pen example. It's true that the microexpectation that the pen would write for six months was set by the store clerk, not by the pen manufacturer. Now the manufacturer could throw up its hands and say: "What can we do about what the store clerks say to customers?" As it happens, there are two possible answers to that question: (1) nothing and (2) something. If nothing is done, then yes, it does become something of a crap shoot. If, on the other hand, the pen manufacturer recognizes that the customer is going to judge the pen's quality on the basis of perceptions relative to expectations, and that those expectations can be set by, among other things, store clerks, then the manufacturer might want to take some steps to ensure that people like store clerks set the right expectations. Said another way, the manufacturer can examine the *process* by which expectations are set and take whatever actions are required to tune and refine that process. (For example, the manufacturer might print up a handy reference card called "How to Sell Our Pens Effectively" for use by store clerks.)

Note that it's not a matter of passively sitting back and hoping to hit the customer's expectations. It's a matter of actively getting out there, finding out what the customer's expectations are, and in some cases resetting those expectations to where you want them to be. Consider the Davisson Realty case. I can almost hear Alice Davisson now: "I don't know where the Daltons ever got the idea that we'd call them after every showing. We never talked about any of that kind of thing." Exactly! The reason that the perceived quality of service went south is that a microexpectation was missed. And the reason that the microexpectation was missed is that the issue of expectations wasn't ever considered. No attempt was made to discern and/or set expectations.

It's only after quality is thought of in terms of customer expectations that the standard operating procedures (i.e., the internal/operational specifications) can most effectively be defined. To the extent that this model forces you to consider a set of requirements that might otherwise be missed, the "customer expectations" approach to quality gives you more control, not less.

There's no such thing as a free lunch. People won't want to pay for all those extra touches.

But they're "extra" only if they're not expected. And by definition, those are precisely the things I'm *not* talking about. The Daltons did not consider the follow-up phone calls to be an extra, and when they didn't get the calls, they perceived— and therefore they received—poor quality.

Moreover, I'm not so sure that people aren't willing to pay for extra touches. Suppose, in the middle of their house-selling ordeal, the Daltons had seen an advertisement that read LIST YOUR HOUSE WITH US, AND WE GUARANTEE THAT WE'LL CALL YOU EVERY TIME ANYONE COMES TO SEE IT. Don't you think they might have been interested—even if that realtor had been slightly more expensive? (For those lawyers who are reading this and who remember that the Daltons signed an "exclusive" contract with Davisson Realty, calm down: It's only a hypothetical.)

We've got all we can do to run the business as it is. We can't spend the time or money it would take to manage something so nebulous as "customer expectations."

But isn't that *exactly* what people were saying about quality five or ten or fifteen years ago?

"Of course quality is desirable and important. But we can't afford to do it and still remain competitive."

"I'd love to be able to do it, but I just don't have the resources."

"I'll get to it, but I've got other things that have higher priority right now."

All of which is, to use the technical expression introduced at the beginning of this chapter, "a load of crap."

You can claim that you have all you can do "to run the business as it is," but if running the business is not fundamentally an effort designed to meet your customers' expectations, then where, pray tell, are you running to?

You may think that the notions of (1) spending time setting customer expectations and worrying about perceptions and (2) remaining cost-competitive are mutually exclusive. But let me spring a quick quiz on you: You're in the car business. You have a prospective customer to whom quality is important. Would you rather be trying to sell that customer an American car or a Japanese car? Now ask yourself: Can you separate "perceptions" and "expectations" from competitiveness?

You may think that you "don't have the resources," but you'd run headlong into the oldest quality irony of all: How is it that you don't have the time or resources to do it right, but you do have the time and resources to do it *twice?* Don't you suppose it might have, net, saved Alice Davisson some time, effort, and money to have taken the time and effort to set clear expectations with the Daltons up front? Had she been clearer about just what the process would be by which she would sell their house, a lot of quality problems could have been avoided. Had she said, "We will give you a follow-up call only if somebody shows interest in your house," the Daltons would have been left with two choices. They could have said OK, in which case the whole issue would have gone away. Or they could have said: "We'd really like to be called whenever someone sees the house." That would have left Alice Davisson with two choices. She could have said OK, in which case the whole issue would have gone away. Or she could have discussed the matter with the Daltons and worked out a mutually acceptable solution. In which case, the whole issue would have gone away. The point, of course, is that the only way of ensuring that all the issues are dealt with is to deal with them—as soon as possible. Which is just another way of saying that it's always better to design the quality in than to detect and repair quality problems after the fact. Which sounds a lot like the quality orthodoxy to me.

If you've got higher priorities than "meeting your customers' expectations," you're in a whole lot more trouble than any book is going to bail you out of. Time and effort spent actively managing your customers' expectations is time and effort spent actively managing quality. And time and effort spent actively managing quality is time and effort spent actively staying in business. So the customer expectations approach would seem to be worth more than a passing glance. The fundamental problem between Davisson Realty and the Daltons was a mismatch between what Davisson's internal/operational specifications were designed to enable it to do—that is, to sell houses—and the Daltons' expectations for Davisson Realty—expert advice, hand holding, counseling, and just-general-being-there throughout the whole, difficult process of selling their house. Davisson Realty wasn't in the business of providing what the Daltons were after. The Daltons hadn't bought what Davisson Realty was equipped to deliver. It was more or less inevitable that problems would arise. At this point it's too late for the Daltons to change the process by which they sold their house. It's not too late for Alice Davisson to change the process by which she sells houses. Unless, of course, it is.

✳ ✳ ✳

What it ultimately comes down to is this: Problems involving broken expectations are not "like" quality problems, or "analogous to" quality problems, or "similar to" quality problems. They *are* quality problems, and they're every bit as real and *every* bit as damaging as broken products themselves.

Over the past several years I have argued this case to thousands of different people from hundreds of different companies in dozens of different industries. And the most common question or objection that comes up is this: "We've made a lot of progress by realizing that quality is something that can and must be managed—that it's within our control. Doesn't the expectations approach let the genie back out of the bottle? Doesn't it undo all our progress by making quality completely abstract and nebulous again?"

But the reality is that customer expectations exist whether you decide to do anything about them or not. Moreover, customers make purchase decisions on the basis of those expectations. It's all they have to go on. It's the luxury for which they're paying by being a customer. (And you can be sure that that's the case, because you are a customer dozens of times every day and you know you make decisions exactly that way.)

Coming to the insight that quality is measurable and manageable in internal/operational terms represents significant progress. It transforms a number of variables that initially seemed beyond control into specific parameters that are not only well within an organization's control but also right at the core of its responsibilities.

"Customer expectations" are abstract and nebulous only if they are viewed that way. All I'm suggesting is that it is much more hard-edged and realistic to recognize them as another set of parameters that must—and *can*—be managed, as another set of requirements to which you can—and *must*—conform. Because to the customer, there isn't a damn thing that's abstract or nebulous about expectations. And the customer has all the votes when it comes to quality.

Business Beat:

The Quality Tradesperson of the Year

[*The setting is a TV studio. The set: two easy chairs, a coffee table, and an assortment of potted palms. The show is called "Business Beat." Its host, Robert Fielding, and its guest, Raymond LaPointe, are seated in the easy chairs. As the final notes of the show's theme music are played, Robert looks into the camera and begins.*]

ROBERT: Good evening. And welcome to "Business Beat." I'm Robert Fielding, and I'll be your guide through the world of interesting persons whom we hope will be personally interesting for the person we're most interested in: you. Our guest on today's program is Raymond LaPointe, and he's here because he's just been named the Quality Tradesperson of the Year for all of Irvington County.

RAYMOND: Actually, it was for the entire tri-county area.

ROBERT: [*Obviously impressed*] Welcome, Raymond, and congratulations.

RAYMOND: Thank you very much.

ROBERT: Tell me, Raymond: Quality Tradesperson of the Year. Just how was this decision arrived at? Who made the selection?

RAYMOND: Robert, the reason this award means so much to me is that it was based on the votes of the only people whose judgment really matters—the customers.

ROBERT: You mean it was a sort of survey or something?

RAYMOND: That's right. Thousands of names were selected at random, and they were asked to name the tradesperson in the tri-county area whom they most liked to do business with. I'm very proud to say that I was named by 64 percent of those responding.

ROBERT: 64 percent! That's very impressive.

RAYMOND: [*Pleased*] The runner-up got 7 percent.

ROBERT: 64 percent to 7 percent. That's quite remarkable.

RAYMOND: Well, thank you. [*He chuckles.*] The joke around the office is that those other 7 percent wouldn't know a quality tradesperson if one bit him! [*He breaks up laughing.*]

ROBERT: [*Politely smiling*] Sounds like you not only do your job well, but have fun doing it.

RAYMOND: Oh, you gotta, you gotta. Life is too short, that's what I always say.

ROBERT: Yes, well, Raymond . . . if I were one of your customers, just what kind of service might I be calling you for?

RAYMOND: Pretty much anything, actually.

ROBERT: Anything?

RAYMOND: Uh, huh.

ROBERT: Like plumbing?

RAYMOND: Oh, yes. We get a lot of calls for plumbing work.

ROBERT: Electrical work?

RAYMOND: Oh my, yes. Electrical bookings are key to us.

ROBERT: Masonry?

RAYMOND: Yup.

ROBERT: Painting?

RAYMOND: Oh, yes.

ROBERT: Carpentry?

RAYMOND: [*Nodding*] Carpentry.

ROBERT: Heating and air conditioning?

RAYMOND: Absolutely.

ROBERT: Wallpapering?

RAYMOND: [*Nodding*] Wallpapering.

ROBERT: [*Searching*] Window treatments?

RAYMOND: [*Nodding*] Window treatments.

ROBERT: [*Still searching*] My goodness—is there anything I've missed?

RAYMOND: Let's see . . . did you say ceramic tile and grout work?

ROBERT: No, I didn't.

RAYMOND: Well, there's a lot of call for that, too.

ROBERT: This is all very remarkable. After all, becoming an accomplished tradesperson in any one of those fields usually takes a lifetime of work. Yet 64 percent of the people in the tri-county area seem to be saying that you've mastered them all. How do you do it? What's your secret?

RAYMOND: There is no secret to quality, Robert. Although I guess "caring" is what matters most.

ROBERT: And just how much time each day do you put in on the job "caring"? I bet it's an extraordinary amount.

RAYMOND: Oh, an hour. On an especially busy day, maybe an hour and a half.

ROBERT: Well, that *is* extraordinary—although not in the way I thought it would be.

RAYMOND: Don't confuse quality with quantity, Robert.

ROBERT: But only an hour and a half each day. Come on now . . . you must have a *few* secrets you can share with our viewers. Things you've picked up over your years in the business.

RAYMOND: Years?

ROBERT: Yes, years. [*Raymond's reaction clearly signals that "years" doesn't apply to him. This does not pass unnoticed by Robert.*] Just how long have you been in business?

RAYMOND: Next Tuesday, the sixth of the month, we'll celebrate eight glorious months in business!

ROBERT: Eight months?

RAYMOND: [*Proudly*] That's right.

ROBERT: And you're the Quality Tradesperson of the Year?

RAYMOND: That's what the people say.

ROBERT: And you've mastered all those trades?

RAYMOND: Oh, no. Of course not. It takes a lifetime to master those things, you know.

ROBERT: I know. That's what makes it so amazing that you've become, for example, a master carpenter.

RAYMOND: Master carpenter? Me? [*Explosive laughter*] I wouldn't know a hammer if it bit me!

ROBERT: Plumber?

RAYMOND: [*Another laugh*] Oh, no, no, no.

ROBERT: Mason? [*Guffaws from Raymond*] Electrician?

[*More guffaws*] Ceramic tile and grout work?

RAYMOND: [*Laughing uncontrollably*] Oh, stop, please! You're killing me!

ROBERT: But you said you do all those things.

RAYMOND: [*Wiping his eyes, composing himself*] No, I didn't. I said that I got a lot of calls for those things, and I booked a lot of that business. I don't actually *do* any of that sort of work.

ROBERT: I don't understand.

RAYMOND: [*A final dab at this eyes*] Ah . . . look—what's the biggest complaint you hear about tradespeople?

ROBERT: That you can never get one when you need one?

RAYMOND: Right. Well, you call me for an appointment, you get an appointment.

ROBERT: But what happens when your appointment book fills up?

RAYMOND: Doesn't matter.

ROBERT: Doesn't matter?

RAYMOND: Doesn't matter. And if you wanna know why, answer me this: What's the second biggest complaint about tradespeople?

ROBERT: I don't know.

RAYMOND: Sure you do. Come on—think about it.

ROBERT: That they don't show up when they say they're going to show up?

RAYMOND: And . . . ?

ROBERT: And . . . they don't even have the courtesy to call and say they'll be late?

RAYMOND: Or aren't coming at all!

ROBERT: I suppose so. Or not coming at all.

RAYMOND: So that's it. I said that there were no secrets, but I guess that I do have one, and that's it.

ROBERT: I'm sorry. I must be missing something.

RAYMOND: That's OK. You and everybody else in the trades. You call me for any kind of work—plumbing, electrical, painting, whatever—you got it. You want to book me for first thing on the morning of the tenth? Bang: It's done. Booked.

ROBERT: But you never actually do the work . . . ?

RAYMOND: Hell no. It takes a lifetime to master those things. Next Tuesday, God willing, I'm in business eight months.

ROBERT: But 64 percent of the people rated you best . . . ?

RAYMOND: Because I call to tell them I won't be there.

ROBERT: All the time?

RAYMOND: All the time.

ROBERT: That's it?

RAYMOND: That's it. I'm serving a niche market.

ROBERT: You mean "people who never wind up getting the work done but are pleased that you called"?

RAYMOND: [*Delighted*] Now you got it!

ROBERT: Don't tradespeople usually get paid upon the delivery of their service?

RAYMOND: Usually, that's right.

ROBERT: So isn't cash flow a problem for you?

RAYMOND: You've got to pay your dues. I'm not one of those operators out to make a fast buck. I'm building a business here. Referrals are everything in this line of work.

ROBERT: Yes, but you don't actually *do* anything, and you don't get *paid* anything.

RAYMOND: Up until now, I haven't gotten paid. But with this award . . . we're ready to roll out an entire menu of services.

ROBERT: For instance.

RAYMOND: Well, for a standard price, we guarantee that we'll call anywhere from twenty-four to forty-eight hours in advance and tell you we can't make the appointment. But some people need more notice. They can pay us a 10 percent premium, and we'll give them a full week's notice. For 20 percent: two weeks' notice. And for a 30 percent premium, we'll give you a full month's notice. I know it costs a lot, but people will pay for quality.

ROBERT: Well, this is quite an interesting concept. And the possibilities are even more remarkable seeing as how you're not limited by, well . . .

RAYMOND: By actually having to have some skills and all?

ROBERT: Yes, I suppose that's the notion I was groping for.

RAYMOND: You're very insightful, Robert. Most people focus on the obstacles, not the opportunities. But you see, it's these other people's shortsightedness that provides the biggest opportunities of all.

ROBERT: Any plans for expansion?

RAYMOND: As a matter of fact, yes. Beginning next year I will be offering my services on a contract basis to other tradespeople. That will enable them to be out there every day doing good, honest work and getting hopelessly behind in their schedules. For a monthly fee, I'll . . .

ROBERT: You'll call up their customers and say they won't be there.

RAYMOND: Exactly.

ROBERT: [*Incredulous*] Amazing.

RAYMOND: [*Oblivious*] Thank you. And you know, there's nothing that says I have to stick to the trades. I mean, who else is famous for falling behind in schedules?

ROBERT: I don't know . . . judges? The courts?

RAYMOND: Hey, I hadn't thought of that! [*Writing*] The courts. That's good! I was thinking about doctors.

ROBERT: You sell the same sort of service to doctors?

RAYMOND: No, not yet. Haven't paid my dues like I have in the trades. I have to establish a practice first. Of course, the barriers to entry are considerably lower since things like medical school don't really have to enter into it. I figure that eighteen, twenty-four months out I'll be locked in to all the medics in the tri-county area.

ROBERT: Well, Raymond, we're almost out of time. Is there anything else you'd like to tell our viewers?

RAYMOND: As a matter of fact, there is, Robert. [*Into camera*] I feel blessed to have been born in the wonderful country, where someone like myself, with no training, no experience, and no discernible skills to speak of, could win as prestigious an award as this [*Holds up quality award*]. Now I'd like to give something back. I'd like to announce that beginning next month, I will be offering a series of seminars in which I will share with you the ideas that have gotten me to where I am today. We will be holding seminars in New York, Washington D.C., Atlanta, Dallas, Los Angeles, and San Francisco. The price for this one-day seminar is just $295. If you'd like to register, just call the number appearing on the screen now: 1-800-555-1111. That's 1-800-555-1111.

ROBERT: What about Chicago?

RAYMOND: Chicago? What about it?

ROBERT: Oh, nothing. It's just that Chicago is usually one of the cities included on lists like that. You know—it's usually New York, Washington, etc., etc., etc., *and Chicago.*

RAYMOND: You think that we should be in Chicago, too?

ROBERT: *I* really don't care. It just would seem to make sense to be in Chicago. Big population. Centrally located.

RAYMOND: You're right. [*To camera*] Ladies and gentlemen, it gives me great pleasure to add another city to our list of seminar sites: Chicago! We'll be in the windy city on, uh, the twenty-fifth. Yes . . . the twenty-fifth. So mark that date down.

ROBERT: [*He has caught on.*] You're not going to be doing

any seminars, are you—that's why you could add Chicago to the list so easily, right?

RAYMOND: Well, no, you're right. But like I said before: You gotta pay your dues.

ROBERT: And the $295 for one day—that's just a come-on, isn't it?

RAYMOND: New business, seminars. Market share is key. And besides, nobody will have to pay it. They'll all get phone calls telling them the seminar was cancelled. I guarantee it. And with plenty of notice, too.

ROBERT: [*Over Raymond*] Well, that's about all we have time for. I'd like to thank Raymond LaPointe, this years's Quality Tradesperson of the Year for the entire tri-county area.

RAYMOND: Thank you for having me, Robert. And as a token of my appreciation, may I offer you free admission to one of my seninars?

ROBERT: [*Skeptical*] Yeah, right. I want to go to the one in Guam.

RAYMOND: Guam? [*Pause*] You've got it. Guam!

ROBERT: [*Still more skeptical*] And I want it to be tomorrow.

RAYMOND: Whoa, tomorrow! OK, OK. Tomorrow it is. But there's just one thing. Why don't you give me your home phone number . . . just in case I might have to give you a call or something.

ROBERT: Sure, sure. Off the air. [*To camera*] And so good-bye until next time on "Business Beat," when we bring you back to the world of interesting persons whom we hope will be personally interesting for the person we're most interested in: you.

[*Closing theme. Credits*]

RAYMOND: [*Under credits*] Thanks for that idea about the courts and judges. That could be a whole new market for me.

[*Fade out*]

Yet Another
Quality Quandary

If a tree falls in the forest
And there is no one to hear it
But somebody paid good money, expecting to hear it:
Is there a sound? And if so, what is its quality?

4

"You Make a Great Product . . . It's Too Bad We Have to Do Business With You"

So quality is "that which meets the customer's expectations." The question is: Expectations for what? What is the "it" the quality of which is so important?

Consider the marketing bromide: "People who buy 1/4-inch drill bits don't want 1/4-inch drill bits; what they want is 1/4-inch *holes.*" They aren't buying a product so much as the answer to a need: how to get 1/4-inch holes into a piece of plywood.

As it happens, in this case the answer is relatively straightforward. The customer drives to the hardware store, parks the car, locates the drill bits in the store (perhaps stopping to ask a store clerk for directions), selects the drill bit from the display racks, stands in line at the checkout counter, and pays for the purchase. In short, the need is answered by engaging in a *transaction.*

The transaction described above is not terribly unusual. Customers understand that that's the sort of routine they have to go through. They *expect* to engage in all the various elements of the transaction.

So if quality is a function of expectations, and customers

have (unarticulated) expectations for the entire transaction, doesn't it stand to reason that the "it" the quality of which is so important ought to be *the quality of the total transaction?*

Think of all the places where quality problems might arise during the drill bit transaction. If the drill bit were defective, there would clearly be a quality problem. But there would also be a (transaction) quality problem if the parking lot were designed so as to make parking a hassle. Or if the store were poorly laid out. Or if the customer had difficulty finding a clerk who knew where the drill bits were located. Or if the customer had to wait too long (and the definition of "too long" is purely up to the customer) in the checkout line. Or if the customer were given the incorrect change. Or if the bag tore open on the way out to the parking lot. (Don't ask me; maybe the customer needed 1,000 1/4-inch drill bits.) Or any of a hundred other things that are part of the overall experience of engaging in a transaction and that, therefore, can go wrong.

Isn't all this a little on the obvious side? Yes and no. It's obvious *if* you take the time to consider it. But how often do you, as the supplier of goods and services, take that time? Discussions about quality tend to focus on the quality of the *product* or the *service* itself. That's perfectly natural, perfectly understandable. Particularly when you spend forty-plus hours at work each week designing, or building, or delivering those products and services. But it's not the focus that your customers have; it's not *really* what your customers are buying. They're buying an answer to a need, and to do that they're engaging in a transaction. And their overall perception of quality—the quality of the total transaction—will determine their purchase decisions. That's the reality of the situation, and it's exactly analogous to extending the definition of quality beyond internal/operational specifications:

- You deal in specifications; your customer *feels* expectations.
- You deal in products and services; your customer *feels* answers to needs.

Clearly, an important element of the quality of a transaction is the quality of the product or service itself. I'm merely making an arithmetic point. If your total focus is on the quality of the product or service you offer, then you are much more likely to overlook areas of potential quality problems (or—let's be optimistic—quality improvement) throughout the rest of the transaction. And that overlooked quality problem might have just as big an impact on a customer as a matter of product quality. "You make a good product. It's just too bad I have to do business with you." That's the sound of a customer with a serious quality complaint talking about a business with, therefore, a serious quality problem.

Now, you might look at the drill bit example and think: "But that's a retail store. The drill bits were made by another company altogether." And you'd be right, but the point is that the customer wouldn't really care. Customers aren't likely to make distinctions between who built the drill bit and who sold it to them. (If they do make such distinctions, they're doing you a very big favor, since they've paid for the right not to have to worry about such things.) More than likely, the customer will come away from a bad transaction thinking: "God, that was awful!" And that can't be good for either Ajax Hardware or Acme Drill Bits.

It's also a caution to the Acme Drill Bits people not to take too much solace in the fact that merchandising their products is "not their job." It's true that some customers will not hold Acme accountable for Ajax's shortcomings; it's also true that some *will* hold Acme accountable. Acme's reputation (and sales) will suffer because of the quality of the overall transaction delivered by Ajax. Is that fair? Absolutely; the customer paid for that privilege. What should Acme do about it? Whatever it takes to work with Ajax to ensure that people associate transaction quality with Acme products. In the extreme case that might mean refusing to have products stocked at Ajax Hardware.

Let's look at an example where this (spectacularly uninteresting to the customer) distinction between "who built it" and "who merchandised it" doesn't exist.

✳ ✳ ✳

You run a small (one-person) business out of your home. Because of the nature of that business, reliable telephone communication is absolutely essential to you. (I don't know. Maybe you're a bookie.) So you buy a new telephone unit, one with all kinds of fancy features and gewgaws and bells and whistles. About three weeks after you purchase the phone, you begin to notice static on the line. It doesn't always happen. But it happens often enough to be a problem. Besides, the phone is almost brand new and it just shouldn't be behaving that way. So you send it to the manufacturer (the service address is listed in the booklet that came with the phone) for warranty repair. You use your old phone unit as a backup in the meantime. It doesn't have all the bells and whistles of your new phone, but it will have to do. (For those troubleshooters out there, let's go on record with the fact that you plugged three other phones from other parts of your house into the new phone's wall jack, and the static problem never occurred. That suggests that the problem is in the new phone and not in the line.)

Now let's look at a couple of different ways in which the rest of this transaction might unfold.

Scenario 1. Seven weeks after you send your phone in for repair, it is shipped back to you by the manufacturer's service department. In the box is your phone (the serial number matches the one you have in your records), packing material (the clear kind with the bubbles that your kids like to make pop), and a pink piece of paper (some sort of packing slip with information that may be important to the manufacturer but that means nothing to you). You take the phone out of the box, plug it into the wall jack, and place a call to the time/temperature operator, who tells you that "at the tone the time will be ten . . . thirty-eight . . . and twenty seconds. Temperature . . . seventy-two F . . . twenty-two C." There is no static. The phone *seems* to be working better than it did before. You think.

Scenario 2. Five days after you send the phone in for repair, you receive this card in the mail from the manufacturer's service department:

We have received the Model Number A-505 that you sent us. We will examine the unit to identify the source of the "line static" problem that you described in your letter and take whatever steps are necessary to eliminate the problem. We expect to ship the repaired unit back to you within the next six to eight weeks. If the shipping schedule should differ significantly from that projection, we will inform you of that fact. In the meantime, if you have any questions, please don't hesitate to call at the number listed above.

Seven weeks from the day on which you sent the phone out for repairs, it arrives back at your house. In the box (along with the packing slip and packing material) is a brief note, describing the nature of the problem that had been isolated and the repair steps that had been taken. You take the phone out of the box, plug it in, and place a call to the time/temperature operator. There is no static. You're *sure* the phone has been fixed.

In both scenarios, the phone is returned without, it would seem, a static problem, suggesting that the "product quality," in the usual sense in which the phrase is used, was the same. The delivery time, a common proxy for "service quality," was the same. But as the customer, you somehow feel that Scenario 2 is better. What you are reacting to is the fact that there was a better match between what you got and what you expected. In short, you perceive better quality—better transaction quality—as a result of your expectations having been actively and effectively managed.

Customers don't buy products or services; they seek out answers to needs. What, given the nature of your business, did you need? A phone? Yes, but that's not all. In a word, what you needed was *confidence* in your phone, and that confidence was lacking because of the intermittent static problem. What step did you take to seek out an answer to your need? You sent the phone in for service. How confident were you that the phone had been repaired? In Scenario 1 it appeared to be working better, but you really couldn't *know* since it had been an intermittent problem to begin with and the manufacturer did not tell you what, if anything, had been done to resolve it.

Overall sense of "what it felt like to do business with the manufacturer of the phone"? Fair.

Overall sense of perceived quality for the transaction as a whole? Fair.

From your point of view as a customer, Scenario 2 was better. Why? Just a few small touches. The manufacturer sent you a note that your phone had been received, thereby alleviating any doubts that might have cropped up five or six weeks later. (In other words, *preventing* a transaction quality problem before it occurred.) It was a nice subtlety that the note mentioned the static problem, thereby signaling to you that your letter had been read, that "people had listened." The manufacturer explicitly set your expectations for how long the repairs would take, and told you that you would be notified of any substantial variance from that promised delivery. In effect the manufacturer said: "We have taken ownership of the problem. It is now in our hands." What you as the customer perceived was: "This company has its act together." What you felt was confidence. And that is what you were after, what you expected. The quality of the transaction was perceived as better.

Those things don't happen by accident. If your mind set as a supplier is that you and your company provide "products and services" and your customers buy "products and services," your focus will be on the quality of those products and services, and your actions will tend to follow those described in Scenario 1. But you can also adopt another mind set:

- Quality must be viewed from the customers' perspective.
- Customers are looking for answers to needs.
- Customers seek out those answers by engaging in transactions.
- Therefore, it's the quality of the transaction—a superset of product quality or service quality—that should get the attention.

With this mind set, the answers that you provide will be more similar to Scenario 2. The quality of transactions that you offer will be better managed. Your customers will notice and act on that difference. And you will be amply rewarded.

* * *

Customer A was having difficulty getting her new personal computer software package to do what she wanted it to do. She'd read through the documentation and made several attempts to run her application, but it was no use. She looked at her watch. It was 4:55 P.M. Although she was frankly tired of dealing with the matter, she hated the idea of leaving work for the night with the problem unresolved. So she picked up the phone and called the software company's toll-free 800 customer service number.

"Thank you for calling UserFriendly Software," came the recorded message. "All our customer service lines are busy at the moment. Please hold the line so that the next available customer service representative can assist you."

Customer A sighed, but she wasn't really surprised. She figured it's what she deserved for waiting until the end of the day. Cradling the phone on her shoulder, she sifted through some of the notes she had generated during her futile attempts to get the program working.

"Thank you for calling UserFriendly Software . . ." The same recorded message was repeated over the line. "Well," thought Customer A, "at least I know I haven't been cut off."

In fact, she was reassured that she hadn't been cut off at regular, thirty-second intervals. Ten times. Customer A was no longer reassured by the message. Now she was beginning to get annoyed by it. Then she heard some clicking and switching sounds.

"Aha," she thought. "something's happening."

She was right. A different recording began: "You have reached the Customer Service Department of UserFriendly Software. Our business hours are from 8:30 A.M. to 5:00 P.M. When you hear the beep, please leave your name, telephone number, and a brief description of the nature of your call. That way we can have the person who is best suited to serve you return your call in the morning. Thank you for calling UserFriendly Software."

It was, as it happened, 5:00, closing time for the day at UserFriendly, at which time Customer A was not feeling terribly friendly at all, only a little bit used.

✳ ✳ ✳

When Customer B moved to a new house five months ago, he went through the wonderful experience of sending change-of-address notifications to, roughly, everyone in the world. So by now almost all his mail was coming directly to his new address without a detour past his old one.

Except, that is, correspondence from his car insurance company. Oh, he had sent the company a change-of-address form all right, but his insurance bills kept going to his old house. Now, each of those bills had a little box on the front labeled PLACE AN X HERE IF THE ADDRESS ON THE BILL IS NOT YOUR CURRENT ADDRESS. Customer B had dutifully placed an X in the box and written his new address IN THE SPACE PROVIDED. To be more specific, he had done so five times, with each subsequent monthly bill. So when the latest bill came, still addressed to his ever-older residence, he paid it. But because he happened to be in a pretty ornery mood at the time, he stapled his check to a note that read: "I have been telling you for six months now that I have moved, but you keep sending these bills to my old address. Either change your records to reflect the fact that I've moved or take the little box and the space provided off your bills. I'm apparently wasting my time filling it out each month, and I don't like to have my time wasted."

Customer B didn't really think that his note would have an effect at the insurance company, but it did make him feel better to blow off a little steam—and that, he supposed, was worth something. Then he got a call from his insurance agent.

"What kind of poison pen letters are you sending to Compassionate Mutual?" asked the agent, with a chuckle. He and

Customer B had been friends for years, and he liked to pull his leg.

"Why? Are they giving you a hard time because of me?"

"Not really. But Marie from customer service just called me and said you were being kind of a pain in the ass. She asked me to tell you that they know your address has changed. It's been entered into the system—whatever that means—and the change should be taken care of within the next month or two."

"But it's been six months already. That means it takes them eight or nine months to change an address!?!"

"I know, I know. But Marie wanted to make sure that you knew your messages have been received. All six of them, in fact."

"I see. So they haven't been ignoring me. They're just incompetent."

"Yeah, something like that."

"Oh, good. Now I feel a lot better."

"I thought you might."

✳ ✳ ✳

The telephone repair case, the UserFriendly Software case, and the insurance company change-of-address case all have a number of things in common. First, they're all real-life cases. The names of the companies have been changed (to protect the guilty, as it were), but the relevant facts are true. (For the record, in the telephone repair case, the customer encountered Scenario 1—no card, no note, no anything.) Second, I know the people to whom they happened. Third, they all occurred within one random three-month period. The point here is that there's nothing terribly unusual about such stories. They happen to the people around us all the time.

Often the customer, driven only by a personal perception of a situation, may react in a way that seems out of proportion to the facts of the case. But is it really out of proportion?

So Customer A got "hung up on" by UserFriendly's telephone system. That's an easy process fix to make—a trivial change in the way the timers and recordings are programmed. And when a company has a name like UserFriendly Software, you can bet that there will be people in the customer service department who will say things like: "But 8:30 A.M. on day *n* is logically only five minutes later than 4:55 P.M. on day *n* − 1. So what's the big deal?" (To which the only "logical" response is: "Thank you for your input, Mr. Spock.") But to the customer it *is* a big deal, an egregious quality error. Anyone who has spent a day like the one Customer A spent knows exactly how it feels. And the level of seriousness of the error is directly proportional to the tendency of people in the organization to ask: "What's so serious?"

So Customer B had his auto insurance bills sent to the wrong address. "So what? He still got them, didn't he? What does he care that it takes a while for the address change to get into the system? Into *our* system!" But it isn't so much that Customer B cared about the address change. It's that, after six months' time, he was exasperated enough to test the insurance company. And it failed the test. What kinds of doubts did that introduce into Customer B's mind? He might well have concluded something like: "If Compassionate Mutual has this much trouble making a simple address change, I shudder to think what it would be like if I ever have to file a claim!" And what effect might such thoughts have on the likelihood of the insurance company getting repeat business from Customer B? Or on the likelihood that Customer B will recommend Compassionate Mutual to others?

Again, fixing the problem with "the system" might be a fairly straightforward matter. But it's a fix that will be made only if the transaction quality problem is recognized as being as serious as it really is. That is to say, it will be fixed only if the insurance company is concerned that its customers—and its agents—are laughing at them. From the evidence at hand, that's not likely to happen. Customer B had done the company a favor by complaining, and it's safe to assume that others "out there" had noticed that the system was (let's be kind) "deliberate"—that others had engaged in transactions with Compassionate Mutual and been left with a similar sense of "how hard it is to do business with those people." To top things off, the insurance company returned the favor by calling the agent and asking him to get Customer B to lay off. Not the kind of approach that will lead to improved quality.

A third similarity among these cases is that they deal with either service businesses (insurance) or with the service arm of "make and sell" businesses (telephone equipment and personal computer software). But make no mistake: Just as transaction quality is about more than product quality, so it's about more than service quality. The next chapter presents a more detailed discussion of how all functions in all departments in all kinds of businesses can have an effect on transaction quality, and therefore play a key role in delivering quality to customers.

For now, a quick summary:

- Customers have all the votes when it comes to quality.
- Quality is that which meets the customer's expectations.
- Customers have expectations for more than the products or services themselves; they have expectations for the entire transaction. Therefore, they perceive quality in terms of the overall quality of the transaction.
- Customers are not interested in making distinctions between intraorganizational functions or departments; that's what they pay organizations to worry about.
- Customer perceptions are based on *every* contact with the business organization regardless of where in the organization that contact might have originated.
- *Under the circumstances, it behooves organizations to think in terms of the delivery of transaction quality.*

"The Dog Ate My Homework"

[*When last we left the Daltons, Ben and Marcia, they had just moved into their new house on North Street. It turns out to be pretty much everything they had hoped for. But after spending about three months in the house, they decide that it is lacking one important feature.*]

MARCIA: We realized that we should have had an alarm system installed before we moved in. Not that the house is anything fancy. And God knows a burglar would go out of business fast trying to make a living on us. But Ben travels a lot, and I'm here with the kids—including the new baby— and this house is a lot more secluded than our old one was. We just decided that we'd feel better about things with an alarm system.

BEN: It's not cheap. Hell—it's damned expensive. But we figured that what we were buying was peace of mind. I know it's a cliché, but it's true: You can't put a price tag on that sort of thing. It put Marcia's mind at ease, what with me traveling so much and all. And *that* helped to put my mind at ease, too. Once we decided to do it, we figured it didn't make any sense to get anything but the best quality. So I did a fair amount of research into what type of system was the best. Then I called around to see who had had some experience in installing that type of system. Got the name of Jefferson Security Systems. Made an appointment. Dan Jefferson came out and we went through the house. It was a little confusing. But he seemed to know what he was talking about. So we got a price from him, and from one or two others. Those other estimates were more for calibration purposes than anything else. We were pretty sure all along that we were going to go with Jefferson.

[The next week a man from Jefferson Security comes out to install the Daltons' system.]

MARCIA: The installer seemed like a nice enough guy. Pleasant enough, friendly enough. But after a while! If he told me once, he told me a hundred times: "We really prefer to install these systems while the house is being constructed. It's a lot easier for us before the inside walls go up. Now I have to spend a lot of time drilling holes and snaking wires around. It's a real hassle." I mean, I can understand his problem and I suppose that I don't blame him, but even if you assume that I care about how much trouble he was having—which I don't—just what did he expect me to do about it? It's not as though they were doing all that drilling and snaking for free. Anyway, I found it kind of hard to work up a lot of sympathy for his troubles, considering the fact that with his drill going all day long, the baby didn't get any sleep at all. She's going to be a real joy later on tonight.

BEN: Then I come home from work and, you know, I walk around to see how things look. And I go into our bedroom and I see the keypad on the wall. I thought: "Izzat where we said we wanted it?"

MARCIA: It wasn't where we *said* that we wanted it, but it was where they put it. I was downstairs with the kids. The guy from Jefferson was working his way through the house, running his wires, and bitching and moaning. I finally went upstairs and saw where he had installed the keypad. On the wall of the master bedroom instead of in the hallway, which is what was written down on the plans that he had. You know what he said when I pointed out the problem—his mistake—to him? He said: "I can move it out into the hallway, but then you'll have a big hole in the wall of your bedroom."

BEN: Can you believe that? Amazing. Anyway, we talked about it for a while and realized that we could insist that they put the keypad in the hallway where we wanted it, and we were pretty sure that we could get them to pay for the plastering and painting that would be required—I mean it was written in the plans—*their* plans—that it was supposed to be in the hallway. But the more we thought about it the more we began to feel that maybe it would be better in the bedroom after all. Besides, that way we could avoid what we knew would turn out to be a major hassle. I'm getting very good at sensing when hassles are going to happen. The rule of thumb is that while you're in the process of buying or selling a house or getting set up in a new house, the surest sign that a hassle is approaching is that you get up in the morning and think that everything finally seems to be under control. Deadly.

[*A week later, the installation is complete. As is his custom, Dan Jefferson comes out to the Daltons' home to check out the work done by his installer. He gives Marcia a walking tour of the system, pointing out its various features and briefing her on its operation.*]

MARCIA: It's all interesting enough, and it sounded pretty straightforward. But I have to confess that I wasn't exactly hanging on his every word. That's kind of hard to do when you're schlepping a baby around and keeping one ear cocked to know just what the other kids are doing at the other end of the house. So we get to the end of Dan's tour and I thank him and then I ask him to leave the brochure on the kitchen table so I can look it over more carefully when I get a few quiet minutes. Sometime in the early twenty-first century seemed about right. And he says to me: "Brochure? We don't have a brochure." He didn't have anything in print—nothing written down—that described the system's features and operating instructions. He gave me a look like I was this great howling bimbo from Mars. But, you know, a brochure seemed like a pretty reasonable thing to expect. When you pay a lot of money for a system like this, you'd think someone would have bothered to write something down at some point, don't you? Anyway, Dan had to give me another tour. He wasn't too pleased. This time I took notes.

[*Three weeks later, at 4:30 A.M., the alarm goes off. The good news is that the alarm is apparently loud enough to wake up both Ben and Marcia. The bad news is that, if the Daltons' new alarm system is to be believed, someone is trying to get into their house at 4:30 in the morning.*]

BEN: Alarm system or no alarm system, I did just what everybody always does in situations like that. I grabbed something to use as a weapon—I think I picked up a coat hanger. Probably plastic. And I went downstairs, making enough noise so that whoever was down there would have a real good chance to hear me and leave. Either that, I suppose, or a real good chance to jump me. Well, I went through the whole house and found nothing that looked unusual. No windows broken. No doors ajar. No extra people in the house—at least not as far as I could tell. So I went over to the downstairs keypad—the installer put that one where it was supposed to go—and I turned off the sirens that had been going for about five minutes. Then I waited, but there was no phone call.

MARCIA: The way I understood Dan to explain it is that whenever the alarm was set off, Jefferson Security would call our number. If we answered and gave our code number, Jefferson would know it was a false alarm. If nobody answered, or if somebody answered but couldn't give the code number, the police would be sent to the house. Sounds like a good system.

BEN: So now it's the middle of the night and I've got about four gallons of adrenaline running through me and I'm waiting for the phone to ring. Finally I figure the hell with it, and I call the alarm company. A woman answers and I tell her who I am. Then I ask her why she hadn't called. She says: "It came in a 9." I said: "Excuse me?" She says, very defensively: "It came in a 9!" Then I can hear her ask somebody else in the room, again, real defensive and upset: "If it comes in a 9, then I'm not supposed to call back, am I?" Apparently she was right. If it "comes in a 9" she's not supposed to call. So now I'm trying to calm her down: "It's OK. Don't be so defensive. I just thought you would call, that's all. But you have to tell me—what does 'come in a 9' mean?" Well, it turns out that's the code Jefferson uses when the alarm is reset at the keypad. So the alarm had gone off, I had reset it, and that was the signal not to call. That's OK, but I wish I had known. It was crazy. I get rousted out of a sound sleep by an air raid siren going off about five feet away from my head. It's 4:30 in the morning. I've just finished skulking around my house to see whether or not the Manson family has dropped by for a visit, and *I'm* calming *her* down?!?

[*Two weeks later the alarm goes off again. Once again it happens in the middle of the night. And once again it is apparently for no reason. First thing the next morning, Marcia calls Jefferson Security.*]

MARCIA: I asked for Dan and was told that he wasn't in but would get right back to me. It took him three days to return the call. And when he finally did get back to me, he gave me the third degree. "Are you sure that all the windows were closed?" "Yes, Dan, I'm sure," I told him. "Were they locked?" "Yes, Dan, they were locked." "Was anybody downstairs who could have set off the motion detectors?" "No, Dan. Everyone was accounted for upstairs." "Are you sure?" "Well, I don't know, Dan. Maybe Marley's ghost dropped by to watch a little cable. Of course I'm sure!" What bugged me wasn't so much that he was asking questions. It's just that the questions were pretty simpleminded—like he thought he was talking to some moron. And there wasn't even the hint of an acknowledgment that he was three days late in returning my call. Also, it was really clear from his tone that he had already decided that it couldn't possibly be a problem with the system. That *we* must have been doing something wrong. The way we left it was that he said, basically, "If it happens again, call us again." Can you believe that? But I was so angry that I just wanted to get off of the phone.

[*A week later, it happens again.*]

MARCIA: I call and Dan is as nice as can be. It was a Wednesday. He says he'll come out Thursday afternoon. But Thursday comes and goes. No Dan. Friday comes and goes. No Dan.

[*Over the weekend, Ben and Marcia discuss the possibility of switching to another alarm company. They come to two decisions: (1) It really doesn't make any sense to give their business to another company until the warranty on the equipment purchased from Jefferson Security runs out. (2) They will call Jefferson Security on Monday morning and air their grievances, giving Dan one final (and slim) chance to recoup. Not that they have any compunctions about "firing" Jefferson Security. It's just that to do so would add one more hassle to an already overhassled existence.*]

BEN: I was planning to take Monday off anyway. But before I could call Jefferson, he called us. The conversation was a real classic:

"Hello, Mr. Dalton. This is Dan Jefferson. Sorry I didn't get out to your house last week. I tried to call you on Thursday, but your line was busy. Then I tried to call back on Saturday but there was no answer."

"Dan, look. Don't you think it's a little lame to call and say you tried to call on Thursday but the line was busy? I mean—geez!—why don't you just tell me that the dog ate your homework? I'll bet you said that a lot when you were growing up."

"Excuse me?"

"Never mind. Look, Dan, even if I overlook the fact that you missed the appointment that you set with my wife for last Thursday and even if I believe that you tried to call on Saturday but got no answer, it seems to me that there's another day in between Thursday and Saturday."

"Well, yes, but you see—"

"No, Dan, please. Don't explain any more. I don't think I could take it. Look, what's past is past so let's leave it at that. But I just want you to be sure you know you've got a customer who's very annoyed and very unhappy."

"I can understand that, up to a point."

He really said that—"up to a point." By then I didn't know

whether to laugh or to scream. I mean, everything about the way he had handled our situation had been wrong. *Everything!* By now I'm kind of used to this sort of thing, you know? There are all kinds of people in the world who do business this way all the time and think nothing of it, think that there's nothing unusual about it. And the pity is, they're right. There *is* nothing unusual about it.

MARCIA: But the best part is what happened when Dan finally came out. He was at our front door about twenty minutes after he talked to Ben. He was nice and polite but you could tell that he really didn't understand what we were so upset about—that he was humoring us, patronizing us. Anyway, he goes through the whole house, adjusts a few things. He finally acknowledges that maybe, just *maybe*, the connection on one of the doors might have been a little loose and that could have been what caused the false alarms. Anyway, he finishes checking things out, and do you know what he says? He says: "There'll be no charge for this service call!" And when he says it he's all excited, like we're supposed to be so grateful.

BEN: That's not the end of it. Just before he leaves he says to me: "I'm sorry I didn't come out here last Thursday. But I got the message wrong. The guy who took the message got your name confused with 'Donnelly.' You know? 'Dalton,' 'Donnelly.' So that's where the confusion came from." He had forgotten the line he had given me about the busy signals and the no answer and now he comes up with another story altogether! It was priceless. I gotta tell him: "Dan, next time just come right out with it. Tell people, 'The dog ate the phone message.' They'll know it's bullshit. You'll know they know it's bullshit. And they'll know that you know that they know it's bullshit. And that way at least you won't be insulting their intelligence."

MARCIA: That clinched it. As soon as the warranty is up, they're out. They're history.

QUIZ
"The Dog Ate My Homework"

1. What did the Daltons buy?
   a. An alarm system.
   b. An alarm system plus remote monitoring and police dispatching.
   c. Peace of mind.
   d. Dan Jefferson's line about the quality provided by Jefferson Security.

2. Why did the Daltons decide to leave the keypad in the bedroom instead of moving it into the hallway?
   a. They convinced themselves that it would be better to have it in the bedroom.
   b. They didn't want to have the hassle of moving it.
   c. They didn't want to inconvenience the installer.
   d. They were afraid the installer had a brother in the painting and plastering business.

3. The Daltons thought it odd that no printed manual was available. What reason would Dan Jefferson most likely have given to justify this omission?
   a. "The money saved by not preparing a manual enables Jefferson Security to deliver a higher-quality product to its customers."
   b. "The money saved by not preparing a manual makes up for the free service call we gave you."
   c. "It came in a 9."
   d. "The dog ate the press proofs."

4. What did it take for Dan to finally consider the possibility that the problem might have been in his system?
   a. Cool, precise, logical argument.
   b. Manifest physical evidence.
   c. A willingness to give his customer the benefit of the doubt.
   d. Thinly veiled threats.

5. On which half of Dan's brain did Ben's argument finally hit home?

    a. The left half.
    b. The right half.
    c. The missing half.
    d. The half that the dog ate.

6. What aspect of the overall transaction was handled most poorly by Jefferson Security?
    a. The installation.
    b. The monitoring and dispatching.
    c. The service and support.
    d. The ability to remember just who was paying whom for what.

7. What aspect of the overall transaction was handled the best by Jefferson Security?
    a. False.

The Sad, Sad Case of R. Wendell Batson and the Acme Refrigerator Door Magnet Company, Inc.

In which our hero painfully discovers that
the quality of the product
and
the quality of the transaction
may sometimes be poles apart

R. Wendell Batson was the kind of person who prided himself on never—which is to say *never*—missing an appointment. He was a compulsive list maker, always posting a record of the day's appointments on that most conspicuous of places, the door of his refrigerator.

This habit was beginning to get pretty expensive for him, because even though he was familiar with a great variety of fasteners—refrigerator door bolts, refrigerator door spikes, refrigerator door epoxy, refrigerator door solder, and all the other well-known techniques of the day—R. Wendell Batson had not yet heard of the newest breakthrough in refrigerator door adhesives technology: refrigerator door *magnets*.

He looked at the first item on his appointments list ("9:00 A.M.: Refrigerator door replacement to be delivered"), and he sighed. This was the fourth such replacement door in the past year alone. Glancing at his watch, he saw that the serviceman would be there in just twenty minutes. Hardly time to do much of anything. So he picked up a magazine (*Refrigerator Doors Digest*) and began idly flipping through the pages.

So idly, in fact, that he almost skimmed right past an advertisement featuring the headline MAKE THE OUTSIDE OF YOUR REFRIGERATOR AS COOL AS THE INSIDE! Now, that was the sort of headline he saw all the time in this particular periodical. But there, buried deep in the body copy, amidst all kinds of precious wordplay about freshness and perishability and having to go all the way to the North Pole or South Pole to find a better deal, a single word caught his eye.

Magnets.

"Magnets!" exclaimed R. Wendell Batson. "Of course! Refrigerator door magnets!!"

He now raced through the advertisement anything but idly. It was a bit tortuous getting through all the copywriter's snappy patter and turns of phrase, but he finally was able to get to the information he wanted: what the product was (an assortment of refrigerator magnets); what it could do for him (dramatically lower his monthly refrigerator door replacement budget); how much it cost (ten cents per unit, with a schedule of volume discounts); and what he had to do to get one (fill out the order form in the ad and send it in to the manufacturer, the Acme Refrigerator Door Magnet Company).

He got a little annoyed at the size of the order form ("Why don't they ever leave enough room to write out a real, honest-to-goodness address?!?"), but he managed to cram everything into the modest space provided. He ran down the hallway to his desk to get an envelope, a stamp, and a pair of scissors and then walked back to the table where the magazine lay. (People named R. Wendell Batson who never miss appointments also *never* run with scissors.)

After carefully clipping the coupon and slipping it into the envelope, he affixed the first-class postage, licked the envelope's flap, and sealed it with a jaunty rat-tat-tat of his fist.

Turning the envelope right side up, he scanned what was left of the advertisement for the mailing address.

"Where are you supposed to send the thing?" he asked himself. He found out only after tearing open the envelope and transcribing the mailing address from the coupon itself onto another envelope, which he brought back—along with another stamp—from another trip to his desk.

Minor annoyances aside, R. Wendell Batson was a happy man. He could hardly wait to walk down the block to the nearest mailbox and send his order on its way. That he couldn't leave until after the refrigerator door company had come and gone didn't particularly disturb him. "After all," thought R. Wendell Batson, happily, "this is the last such appointment I'll ever have to make!"

✳ ✳ ✳

"Hullo, Acme," said the semi-sedated sounding, seemingly uninterested voice. "Can I help you?"

"Hello. Is this the Acme Refrigerator Door Magnet Company?" asked R. Wendell Batson.

"Yeah," said the voice.

"This is R. Wendell Batson. I sent in an order for a refrigerator magnet some ten weeks ago, and I have yet to receive the order."

"Yeah?" came the less-interested-than-ever response. "Shoulda been shipped by now, you know."

"Yes, I know. That's why I'm calling. Can you help me clear up this problem with your shipping procedures?"

"I doubt it."

"You doubt it?!?"

"Well, I was just thinking. Maybe somebody from the shipping department knows something about your order."

There followed a four-beat pause.

"Well?" demanded R. Wendell Batson.

"Well what?" said the voice.

"Can you connect me with the shipping department?!?"

"Oh, yeah. I suppose so."

"Thank you very much." This was said ironically.

"Don't mention it." This was said obtusely, just before the wrong button was pushed and R. Wendell Batson was cut off.

He dialed the Acme Refrigerator Door Magnet Company for a second time.

"Hullo, Acme. Can I help you?"

"No, you can't, but perhaps the shipping department can. Do you suppose it would be too much to ask you to transfer me?"

"Nope. 'Ats what I'm here for."

This time the connection was made. At least, R. Wendell Batson could hear the phone ringing. And ringing. And ringing. After sixteen rings, a human voice was heard, but the voice was obviously not speaking directly into the telephone.

". . . and then he takes a called third strike! A meatball pitch. Belt high, right over the plate! My grandmother coulda hit it outta the park, and he stands there with the bat on his shoulder! Can you believe it?"

"Hello? Hello?"

"But that's nothing compared to what he does out in the field! Justa minute—I gotta take this call. Hello, shipping."

"Hello? Is this the shipping department?"

"Yeah, that's what I said. What can I do you for?"

"My name is R. Wendell Batson. I placed an order for a refrigerator door magnet about ten weeks ago, and I have yet to receive it."

"What was your order number?"

"Order number?"

"Yeah, the number that's on the upper-right-hand corner of the blue sheet."

"Blue sheet?"

"Don't you have a blue sheet?"

"No—I mean I guess not. I mean, I don't even know what a blue sheet is."

"Then how am I supposed to help you track your order?!?

Hey, Harry! Guy here wants me to track his order and he don't even know what a blue sheet is!"

This last was apparently said to the shipper's baseball discussion companion and was accompanied by a considerable amount of Ralph Kramdenesque har-de-har-har-har'ing.

R. Wendell Batson was partly embarrassed but mostly annoyed. "Look," he said, "I don't know what the order number is, and I don't know what a blue sheet is. What's more—I don't care about those things! All I know is that I placed an order ten weeks ago for a refrigerator door magnet, and I have yet to receive it."

"You'd have to take that up with order entry."

"Order entry? What's that?"

"The department that enters orders," came the oh-so-condescending reply. "Anyways, I can't help you unless you got a blue sheet."

"But you think order entry can?"

"Oh, yeah—yeah, sure. They can help you."

"Well, can you transfer me to the order entry department please?"

"Geez, I dunno how that works. I'll try—I think you're supposed to push this button here. Hey, Harry, how do I transfer this call over to order entry? This is the button I push, right?"

"No, I don't think so," said apparently Harry. Which was the last thing R. Wendell Batson heard, prior to the by-now-familiar sound of a dial tone.

✳ ✳ ✳

As it happens, the people in order entry were not able to help. They would have been, had R. Wendell Batson been able to supply the "shipping zone" number for his order, but he couldn't, so they couldn't.

Neither could the sales department. Or more accurately, neither *would* the sales department. In fact, the person R. W. talked to had scolded him for placing an order through the mail. ("If you'd placed the order through me, I'd have been glad to help out. But you wanted to save a couple of bucks—

take it out of my pocket, from my commission—by placing an order through the mail, you know? Why don't you ask the post office for help? Heh, heh, heh.")

Accounting only wanted to know why, if he had placed the order ten weeks ago, there was no record of his having paid for it yet.

"But I haven't even received the merchandise!"

"Makes no difference. The invoice should have gone out the day after the order was received."

"Even if the product isn't shipped?"

"I don't know anything about shipping the product. Only about seeing that the bills go out on time and get paid on time. Would you like me to connect you to shipping?"

"No!" shouted R. Wendell Batson. But it was too late. He knew in his heart that it would be. And the sound of the dial tone confirmed that judgment.

He decided to place one final call to the Acme Refrigerator Door Magnet Company.

"Hullo Acme. Can I help you?"

"Hello. This is R. Wendell Batson calling—yes, again! I still haven't been able to get the mystery of the missing magnet cleared up. But at this point, I'm not sure I even care. In fact, I have a much more basic question for you. Would you care to try to answer it?"

"S'pose so."

"Good. Just exactly to whom should a customer talk if he desires to receive some service from your venerable company?"

"That would be customer service."

"You have a department dedicated to customer service and you've been passing my call all around your company like this was some sort of relay race?!?"

"Well, did you ever ask for the customer service department?"

"No," answered R. Wendell Batson, in barely restrained, measured tones. "No, I didn't. But I suppose I shall now. Would you be so kind as to connect me to the customer service department?"

"Speaking."

✳ ✳ ✳

Three days had passed since R. Wendell Batson had endured his journey through the telephone switching system of the Acme Refrigerator Door Magnet Company. And in that time (although it *was* rather hard to believe), the customer service representative with whom he had spoken had actually managed to track down his order and set things right.

At least it appeared that way as R. Wendell Batson watched the truck that had just delivered a package from the Acme Refrigerator Door Magnet Company drive off. As frustrated as he had been on the phone seventy-two hours earlier, he was as excited today in his kitchen as he fairly tore upon the box containing his long-awaited refrigerator door magnet.

A veritable antipasto of those little white packing noodles poured out, followed by a yellow invoice marked FINAL NOTICE! wafting down to the floor. R. Wendell Batson dropped to his knees and began digging through the noodles like a hound for a hamster.

Until he found what he was looking for. There, in a small cellophane bag, was . . . *his refrigerator door magnet!* So small, so simple, so—rectangular!

R. Wendell Batson (gently) opened the cellophane bag and took out his prize. Then he looked around for something to try it out on. And since people who never miss appointments also *never* endanger their credit rating, he decided that the perfect thing to affix prominently to his refrigerator door using his new refrigerator door magnet from the Acme Refrigerator Door Magnet Company was the yellow invoice labeled FINAL NOTICE!

He stood in front of his refrigerator door and pressed the invoice flat with his left hand; with his right hand he placed the refrigerator door magnet onto the door of the refrigerator, in between the words FINAL and NOTICE! Then he removed his hands and—the invoice remained affixed to the refrigerator door! No pounding. No gluing. No holes. No damage of any kind whatsoever.

R. Wendell Batson took one step back, the better to drink

in the full effect of his remarkable new possession. So remarkable, in fact, that he all but forgot the long list of hassles and annoyances and inconveniences associated with its purchase.

Then his phone rang.

"Hello?" said R. Wendell Batson.

"This Batson?" came a coarser-than-our-hero-was-accustomed-to-dealing-with voice.

"Er, yes. Who's this?"

"This here's the Acme Collection Agency: a wholly owned subsidiary of the Acme Refrigerator Door Magnet Company. It's my job to get deadbeats like you to pay up."

"Deadbeats? Pay up? For what?"

"For the refrigerator door magnet that you ordered ten weeks and three days ago." If that weren't enough to push R. Wendell Batson over the brink, what followed was: "And for telephone service rendered three days ago by the shipping, order entry, sales, accounting, and customer service departments of the Acme Refrigerator Door Magnet Company. So, Batson, you gonna pay, or what?"

Now, R. Wendell Batson is a gentle man, a kind man. But he had been pushed far enough. The time had come to fight back in the way that the R. Wendell Batsons of the world are wont to do.

"I see," he said, "I see. Well, it seems to me that what you would want is the accounts payable department. Would you hold on while I transfer you?"

"Uh, yeah. I suppose so."

"Thank you *so* much!"

Whereupon R. Wendell Batson—compulsive list maker, appointment keeper, bill payer; dependable as the day is long and predictable as the fact that the day that is so long will also begin to the east; creature of habit and loyal beyond fault, all the way to fetish—hung up on the Acme Collection Agency and its parent company, the Acme Refrigerator Door Magnet Company.

And it is most unlikely that he will ever call back again. Which is a pity, since he found his refrigerator door magnet to be quite a fine product indeed.

Some Ifs, Ands,
or Buts About Quality

If the new gizmo you ordered arrives defect-free
So that gizmo quality's as good as can be,
And the gizmo installer has skills unreproachable
So that "service quality" is a matter unbroachable,
But it arrives a tad late—six months to the day—
In a box that seems to have passed through Pompeii,
While the invoice, of course, has glided right through
(It's the kind of thing kid-gloves handling can do),
And the invoice numbers, though crisp and precise,
Contain a slight defect: they don't match the price,
At least not the price you agreed to when you went into the
store,
And were treated like a bother, and a nuisance, and a bore.

So you call to flag the billing mistake and ask them to
reconsider it,
And are told: "Could you call back after lunch? Could you be
a bit more considerate?"
Then you fuss and fume and wait until two to call back with
your question,
Adjusting your schedule and revising your plans to
accommodate their digestion.
Then you pick up the gizmo manual, triggering your fondest
single wish,
Not that it be shorter or simpler, but that at least it be in
Engl-ish.

When such things happen, are you so discerning, viewing
things with a jeweler's eye?
Do you say "Great product; too bad about your:
    delivery . . .
    and packing . . .
    and sales clerk . . .
    and telephone answering . . .
    and scheduling . . .
    and documentation problems,"
Or do you simply say, "Good-bye"?

5

You're Sending Signals All the Time

"**O**K," some among you may be thinking at this point. "I hear what you're saying about transaction quality, and I don't disagree. Sure, I've been in those kinds of situations. I know what it's like to be the customer and how that feels. But isn't what you're really talking about just customer service? What you're calling transaction quality other people just call quality of service. Aren't they the same thing?"

To which I give an unequivocal: "Maybe." If when you say "quality of service," you broaden the concept of service to comprise *all* contacts with the customer, and if that definition accounts for the effects on the customer of *all* actions taken in *all* functions in *all* departments, then yes—they are equivalent, or at least equivalent enough for our purposes.

But I think most people in organizations hear the word "service" and conclude: "That's the responsibility of the service department." Or of "customer service representatives." Or of anyone else whose job title includes the word "service" or a reasonable synonym (like "customer relations" or "ombudsman"). As a result, they become insulated and separate themselves from any responsibility for "service." And that just won't get it done. (This is precisely equivalent to saying that quality is not just the responsibility of the quality department.)

Transaction quality is everybody's responsibility. So of course those with direct, face-to-face customer contact—like customer service reps, and sales reps, and checkout cashiers— have a huge impact on transaction quality. But there are any number of other ways that organizations come into contact with customers and in the process send out signals as to "what it's like to do business with us."

For example, your company may spend a lot of time and money on advertising. Do those ads present your customers with information that is useful to them? Are the ads clear? Concise? Do they accurately set expectations about what you can deliver? You'd better hope so, because those ads are a very visible (and very expensive) part of the transaction in which your customer is engaged, and if you haven't set the expectations properly—if you haven't designed the quality in—then the money you spend on creating and placing the ads may pale in comparison with what it will cost you to clean up the quality problems waiting down the road. At the moment that a misleading advertisement comes into contact with a customer a defect is introduced into the transaction process. It is cheaper and easier to prevent that defect from occurring in the first place than to detect and fix it after the fact. That's part of the quality orthodoxy as it is commonly applied to products and services. All I'm suggesting here is that the scope be broadened to apply to all aspects of the transaction.

And don't get sucked into the trap of saying: "We would never create ads that were intentionally misleading!" Quality is what happens when what you deliver matches the customer's expectations, not your intentions. The question of intent is not of great interest to your customer. (The same may not be said of your state's attorney general, but that's another issue.) After a problem arises, the customer's reaction (i.e., a willingness to forgive and forget) will almost undoubtedly be colored by your intent—or, to be more precise, by the customer's perception of your intent. But the objective should be "How do we keep the problems from occurring at all?", not

"How can we cut our losses should problems arise?" And that means paying scrupulous attention to the expectations set in your advertising before problems have a chance to arise.

Consider the impression created by the way a company's telephones are answered. Or more to the point, how they're *not* answered. When you call a place of business, don't you have an expectation for how many times the phone ought to ring before it's answered? And long about the sixteenth or eighteenth ring, don't you find yourself thinking: "What's going on here? What kind of place is this to do business with?" And somewhere in the recesses of your mind you file that negative thought away as one data point, one more factor on which you base your sense of "what it's like to do business with these people."

Here's a true story. I was in the lobby of a very high-tech, engineering-driven, our-electrons-move-faster-than-your-electrons-do kind of company, waiting to meet with a representative from the marketing department. I took a seat in the lobby across from the receptionist, who doubled as the company's switchboard operator. Along with greeting visitors, she took all incoming calls and directed them to the appropriate extension. When there was no answer at the extension, she switched on the phone system's intercom and paged the person being called: "Joe Smith, please dial the operator." All pretty routine stuff.

During the ten minutes I spent in the lobby, the receptionist made about three such paging announcements. Each time she did, I noticed that there was a slight rasp or frogginess to her voice. Now, I say that I noticed it, but I didn't exactly fixate on it. It didn't strike me as being anything terribly significant. Until, that is, the receptionist decided to tell me about it: "Whenever I go to page someone, I get this real phlegmy throat and it sounds like this—" Whereupon she made a most unbusinesslike sound involving nasal passages and the back of her throat, and I guess I'll just leave it at that.

What's the point of telling such a repugnant little story? Merely that for all the receptionist knew, I was a customer, or maybe a prospective customer. And the fact is that she had made an impression on me. It was not, shall we say, a favorable impression. Could it have affected a purchase decision that I might have been in a position to make? Absolutely. Understand, it isn't that I would have said to myself: "I have to decide which company will provide my organization with the latest in breakthrough, cutting-edge, crypto-laser-gigabyte technology at a cost of tens of millions of dollars a year for the next six years, and I'm not going to choose this one because the receptionist sounds like a consumption victim." That's not how it happens. The point, rather, is that a negative image had been introduced into my dealings with the organization. A seed of doubt was planted. I might never have made a direct connection to the incident during the purchase decision process. But indirectly, subconciously—*at the margin,* which is where decisions get made—it could well have made a difference.

It may seem illogical that such seemingly irrelevant things can and do make a difference. After all, we're talking crypto-laser-gigabyte technology here. What difference does it make what the receptionist says to people in the lobby or how she says it or what it sounds like? But in reality it is logical as logical can be. An important part of a customer's assessment of a business is based on an overall impression: "Is this a well-managed company? Do I feel a strong sense of competence? Of confidence? How well do these people have their act together?" Under the circumstances, it seems eminently logical for the customer to have certain expectations, to say: "I'm thinking of forking over tens of millions of dollars to you over the next several years. I'm counting on you to be able to manage the incredibly complex, demanding process of developing crypto-laser-gigabyte technology so that it can be applied in a way that meets my needs. You're asking me to put a great deal of faith in you. I would like to think that you have your act together, and my thinking that you have your act together would seem to mean, at a minimum, feeling reasonably sure that your receptionist won't spit up on my shoes." To acknowledge that a customer would have such an expectation is the height of logic. To acknowledge that customers are affected by your performance relative to those expectations is the height of reality.

Consider another point of contact with customers—let's call it ambience. The way the people in a building carry themselves with customers has an effect on perceived transaction quality. You've been in places of business where you are made to feel welcome. You've been in places where it's clear that you're not all that welcome. There is a difference, you perceive the difference, and, over time, you act on your perceptions. I'm not talking about "rolling out the red carpet" or obsequiousness toward customers or anything of that sort. I'm merely talking about the overall set of signals sent to customers—through words, facial expression, attentiveness, body language, whatever—that communicate the degree to which customers are welcome in a business environment.

The physical trappings of a facility also affect perceived transaction quality. Is your facility as neat and organized as it should be for the business that you're in? This is just another way of saying, "Does the appearance of the facility meet your customers' macroexpectation?" No one would expect to be able to eat off the floor of an automobile repair shop. But, since effective automobile care and troubleshooting do require a reasonable capacity for systematic, logical thinking, which in turn suggests the need for a reasonably logical and well-ordered mind, you would at least like to think that the mechanic won't have to spend twenty minutes (at $30 an hour) rummaging through fried chicken bones and tabloid newspapers looking for his socket wrenches before he can work on your car. If, on the other hand, you're about to become the customer of a vascular surgeon, your expectation would be that chicken bones, no matter how neatly disposed of, probably shouldn't enter into the picture at all. Once again, it's not that people stop and pull out a checklist and conduct a thorough inspection of the facilities. That's what they're paying you to worry about. But they are going to have their perceptions—their overall sense of what it's like to do business with you—and it's those perceptions that will determine the level of transaction quality.

Customer invoices are another point of contact. Do your invoices give customers all the information that they might need? Is it presented in an unconfusing way? Is the invoice uncluttered, free of extraneous codes and numbers and who-knows-what-else? Is any action required on the part of the customer clearly spelled out? Was the invoice designed to fit smoothly into the way your customers do business or the way you do business? That is, are the invoices for your customers' convenience or for yours? What department is responsible for creating those documents, for sending those signals to customers?

Every system in your organization deserves the same scrutiny. When customers call to ask about a product's availability, do your customer service reps have a hard time answering because of shortcomings in your information systems? ("Gee, I don't know about your particular order, but if you placed it eight weeks ago it sure seems to me that you should have received it by now, don't you think?") When those shortcomings are identified, do you ignore them because change would be too disruptive to the systems you have in place? Who has responsibility for answering those questions? Who's sending that signal?

When potential customers call to request information about one of your products, do they receive the brochure in the mail in two days? Or in two weeks? Don't you suppose that those different answers send very different signals? Just who is involved in transmitting the signals?

Is your employee orientation program devoted entirely to filling out forms and talking about medical insurance plans and handing out cafeteria menus and telling people where they *must not* park their cars? Or are new employees given the opportunity to learn a little something about your customers and how your organization serves that marketplace? Who has responsibility for answering those questions? What implications do these procedures have for the signals that new hires will eventually send out into the marketplace?

It is commonly said: "Fundamentally, all businesses are service businesses." Although the idea is basically a correct one, I think that in practice its usefulness is limited, because to the extent that it is so commonly accepted, it can become too familiar, too pat. People will stop noticing what's really being said. So I'd like to turn that notion around and suggest a different mind set. I'd like to suggest that *all organizations are, fundamentally, factories*—to be more specific, *transaction factories.* Day in and day out you build transactions for your customers. Their purchase decisions are based purely on the quality of those transactions, which they gauge in terms of their expectations. And all employees, in all departments, in all functions are direct assembly-line workers, adding their piece to the product being built, to the transaction.

Now that can get pretty complicated. So to get our arms around things, let's look at a relatively simple example. Consider a typical twelve-year-old boy—let's call him Jerry—with a typical suburban paper route. To Jerry, his job every morning (including Sunday) is "delivering papers." That's the service that, from his perspective, he provides.

But that's not really all that you as his customer are buying. The morning paper is an important part of your daily routine. You've just awakened. Showered. Dressed. Maybe you're still shaking some cobwebs out as you pour a cup of coffee. You open the front door, pick up the paper, walk back to the kitchen, and begin the day with a pleasant, relaxing interlude. Nice.

But how nice will it be if two days a week the paper isn't there on time? Or if it's not on the front porch, but in the hedges? In a puddle? How nice will it be if, when Jerry comes to collect later that day, he tells you that you owe him for three weeks when you *know* that you paid him last week? (It's one thing to get into an argument with the dunning department of a big credit card company; it's something else again to challenge the accounting acumen of the twelve-year-old kid from down the street.) What about when you go on vacation and tell Jerry to stop delivery for a week, then arrive home to find a pile of yellowed papers on your front step? Etc., etc., etc.

All these things go into determining just how "pleasant" that morning newspaper interlude will really be. And if such things happen often enough, then at some point—it's impossible to predict when it will be, but you'll know it when you've arrived—you will say: "That's enough." You will call Jerry, cancel your newspaper subscription, set your alarm clock fifteen minutes earlier, make a trip to the nearest convenience store each day to buy a paper, bring that paper home, and have a nice, pleasant interlude to start the day. Which is all you were after in the first place. You didn't want to have to do it—but, net, it was better for you.

*** *** ***

As a newspaper delivery customer, what are you after?

A pleasant interlude with which to begin the day.

What factors go into your assessment of the quality of the transaction delivered by Jerry? Specifically, about what sorts of things do you effectively have expectations?

1. *Price.* You are willing to pay slightly more (usually in the form of a tip) for good, door-to-door service.
2. *Time of delivery.* If the paper isn't delivered by 7:00 A.M., you won't be able to read it before going to work.
3. *Days of delivery.* You want the paper every day, including Sunday.
4. *Reliability.* You want the paper in the same place at the same time every day.
5. *Readability.* You would prefer that the paper not be soaked by rain or blown around the yard by wind.
6. *Reasonableness of payment system.* You now pay Jerry $2.50 a week. If he wanted to go to a monthly plan— $10.00 some months, $12.50 others—that would be OK (providing, of course, that the total number of weeks for the year comes out to fifty-two). Suppose, however, he were to say: "Why don't you just give me a check for $130.00 in January and then we don't have to worry

about collection?" You probably wouldn't go for it. ("I mean, what the hell, Jer. Why not an additional $1,300 so we won't have to worry about the 1990s?")

7. *Accurate recordkeeping:* You don't want to be put in a position of arguing with a twelve-year-old kid over $2.50. On the other hand, you don't want to pay him twice each week either.

When you sum all those things up, you will be left with an overall sense of "what it's like to do business with Jerry," an overall sense of transaction quality. (Again, that summing isn't an explicit, item-by-item set of actions on your part. It's far more impressionistic—but no less real—than that.) And on the basis of that perceived transaction quality, you will decide whether to continue to "do business" with Jerry.

That being the case:

What should Jerry do to ensure that he keeps your business?

Above all, he should look at things from your perspective instead of his, and redefine the transaction that is being built in his "factory." Rather than seeing the transaction as delivering papers, he should think of the product he's building as "providing my customers with a pleasant morning interlude." Without question, this is the single most critical step he can take. Just what does it involve in practical, operational terms? What "departments" have a role to play?

The accompanying newspaper delivery chart summarizes some of the considerations involved in providing that pleasant interlude. Before anything can happen, a sale has to be made. Jerry has to advertise, perhaps by putting a hand-drawn flyer into the mailboxes of new people in the neighborhood: "Welcome! If you want the *Gazette* delivered to your door each day, call Jerry, at . . . ." That, in effect, is a *marketing* function.

Jerry might also go out and knock on doors. As such, he is functioning as a *sales* representative.

Product/Service: Newspaper Delivery

Process Steps	Functional Considerations	Responsible Department
☐ Sale Made	☐ Run Ad	☐ Marketing
	☐ Take Order	☐ Sales
	☐ Enter Order	☐ MIS/Accounting
☐ Delivery	☐ Supplier's Schedule	☐ Purchasing
	☐ Route	☐ Design/Planning
	☐ Drop Points	☐ Design/Planning
	☐ Weather Conditions	☐ Planning/Purchasing
	☐ Substitute Carriers	☐ Human Resources
	–Reliable	
	–Competent	
	–Function	
	–Attitude	
	☐ Vacation Stops	☐ Service/Systems/ Planning
☐ Collection	☐ Method	☐ Accounting/MIS/ Finance
	☐ Record Keeping	
	☐ Dunning	

BUSINESS ORGANIZATION

Expectations	Overall "Feeling" of Transaction Quality
☐ Price	
☐ Time of Delivery	
☐ Days of Delivery	"A Pleasant Morning Interlude"
☐ Reliability	
☐ Readability	
☐ Reasonableness	
☐ Re: Payment	?
☐ Accuracy of Record-Keeping	

CUSTOMER

When he gets an order, Jerry somehow has to enter it into his delivery and financial records. Those sound like *systems* and *accounting* functions to me.

So the new customer is signed up. Now delivery has to begin. Jerry has to ensure that he has an additional paper dropped off at his house each day, so he calls his supplier/distributor. When he does, he's functioning as a *purchasing* agent.

Just where in his route does the new address fall? Where does the customer want the paper to be left? Front door? Back door? Side door? To accommodate the new customer, will he have to juggle the order of delivery of anyone else's paper? In answering those questions, Jerry is playing a *design/planning* role.

What's the weather supposed to be like in the morning? Is there any chance of rain? If so, does Jerry have enough plastic bags to protect the papers? How can he be sure to leave himself enough time to bag all the papers while still making the deliveries on time? *Planning* and *purchasing* considerations.

What happens when Jerry is sick? Or when his family goes on vacation? Does he have substitute carriers lined up? Are they reliable? Are they competent? Do they know the route? The deadlines for delivery? The supplier's number? Do they know how to act with customers? Or will they undo months of effort at building good customer relations? To answer those questions, Jerry has to function as a *training* and *human resources* professional.

And what happens when a customer goes on vacation? Does Jerry have a reliable way of keeping track of which deliveries are on temporary hold? And whether the customer wants the papers saved and delivered upon returning from vacation or not delivered at all? Those are *service, systems,* and *planning* roles.

Collection is the last broad process step involved. Does Jerry have a sensible, simple method for collecting payments? Can customers reasonably expect him to show up on, say, Thursday evenings to collect? Or are things handled more haphazardly than that? Does he keep accurate records? When a customer does get behind with payments, does Jerry have a dunning system in place? All those considerations go into the *accounting, MIS*, and *finance* functions.

So when we step back and look at it, what we've got is a twelve-year-old kid who thought that he had a simple paper route but who, if he's going to run a successful business—which is to say, if he's going to deliver the pleasant interlude that his customers are seeking—must run and coordinate the following departments:

- Marketing
- Sales
- MIS
- Accounting
- Purchasing
- Design
- Planning
- Human resources
- Service
- Finance

And any number of others that I've probably overlooked.

On top of all that, Jerry must function as the CEO, by making "the production and delivery of pleasant morning interludes" the clear focus and objective of the organization as a whole. This challenge is rendered easier by the fact that Jerry is a one-man shop and so should have a relatively easy time getting the various department heads to see eye to eye. (Not to mention that achieving a quorum for staff meetings should be a snap.)

In more complex organizations the overall challenge is different—but only in degree, not in kind. Again, organizations like Jerry's and like yours are, in the final analysis, transaction factories. All functions in all departments are part of the assembly line building that transaction.

We all know that all functions in any organization can conceivably do a "better" job. The point here is simply to draw some needed attention to the definition of "better" and to emphasize that "better" in this context means:

- Recognizing that *all* functions have an impact on your organization's performance relative to customer expectations.
- Understanding what those impacts are.

• Doing whatever it takes to ensure conformance with those customer expectations.

Transaction quality is, ultimately, the make-or-break factor for any organization. Conformance to customer expectations for the entire transaction is the key. Your chances for conformance will be much higher if everyone on that transaction assembly line works from the premise that "what I do today in my job—whether it's in sales or marketing or manufacturing or finance or human resources or whatever—will ultimately have an effect on how well we meet our customers' expectations. That's what I'm here for."

One way or another, everyone is sending signals every step of the way.

"Don't They Understand How Much Work Is Involved?"

Medical costs are high and rising. Consequently, the costs of medical insurance are moving in the same northerly direction. No news there. At any rate, it isn't news to Wayne Balducci, Director of Systems Development for The Empathy Groups, Inc. (EGI), a supplier of group medical and dental care plans for small and medium-size businesses. Balducci and his staff of thirty-eight people (comprising programming, administrative, clerical, and marketing support functions) have just completed an extensive product design/pricing overhaul. It has been a major undertaking. According to Balducci:

> We had no choice but to raise our rates. Had to. So what we wound up doing was to offer people a menu of options that they could choose from. In effect, our customers had four choices. They could leave all coverage the same as it was before—for a higher premium, of course. They could keep the same coverage, same premium, but accept a higher annual deductible. They could sign up for the "Prereview Option," which means that before undergoing any kind of major, schedulable procedure, the customer would have to notify us and we would get a chance to review the case

and satisfy ourselves that the procedure was actually warranted. Prereview gives us a little more control over our costs and in return the customer gets a premium reduction. Anyway, the customer can take any of those options, which comes out to four different plans to choose from.

I don't mind telling you that pulling all this together was one colossal job. My people really worked their fannies off, and I'm proud of the job that they did. Once marketing had locked in on what the product and pricing structure was going to be like, we had to document it for our records. We had to prepare the explanatory literature that would be sent out to agents all over the country. We sell through independent agents. Don't have our own sales force. The biggest headache is that we had to modify all our systems to reflect all the changes. Do you have any idea what kind of programming task that is? Nontrivial, to say the least. And while all this is going on, we still have to keep up with business as usual. We don't get to call a moratorium—you know, say to people: "Sorry. We're not going to be processing claims and doing the billing and all that other stuff for the next eight weeks. We have to update our systems." That doesn't work. When you stop and think about what was involved— I just wind up shaking my head. I really still don't believe that we pulled it off.

A week after the price increase notifications went out to EGI customers, Balducci learned of a possible problem with the new pricing structure:

One morning, Sheila—she's one of our programmers, one of our *best* programmers—anyway, Sheila tells me that Ed got a call from one of our agents in the field. Ed is responsible for marketing support. He's the interface between the field and our marketing staff here at headquarters. Apparently there was a customer out there who was squawking because of what he claimed was an "inequity"—that's his word, according to Ed—in our pricing. The customer says that the way we had things set up, he could leave his policy unchanged, keep the same coverage as before, and pay one price. But if he moved to Plan 2—that meant keeping the same deductible amount but adding the Prereview Option—the price for his age bracket went up. He says that doesn't make sense, since it means a higher price for less coverage. And if that were the case, then he'd be right. It would be less coverage for a higher price.

Which is why it *can't* be right. The pricing schedules are encoded in the system and are automatically kicked out by the system, so there's no chance for human error. I told Ed to call the agent back and tell him that the customer must be misinterpreting our pricing charts—tell him to double-check and then call us back if he's still confused. All of which is kind of a pain in the neck to have to do, when you consider what we've gone through over the past couple of months. But there's always one or two cases like this that you have to deal with. It's inevitable.

Those "one or two cases" snowballed into some two dozen cases within the next three days. Calls came in from agents all over the country, citing the same situation: They all had customers in the same age bracket wanting to move to Plan 2, but the customers couldn't understand why the price would be higher than if they stayed on the same plan they were now covered by. In every case, the question was: "Less coverage; higher price—why?" Balducci explains:

It did turn out to be a mistake in our pricing schedules after all. The way we had things set up it didn't really make sense. On the one hand, you ask yourself: "How could this happen?" On the other hand, the answer's obvious: It happens because there's so much to be done in so short a time by so few people. Hell, the way I see it, this was just the exception that proved the rule. My people did a helluva job, and a little problem like this doesn't change that.

The question now is: What are we going to do about it? And the answer is—not a whole helluva lot. Do you realize what would be involved in changing the pricing structure? We'd have to recalculate all the schedules, reprogram all the systems, redo all the literature, resend information packets to our agents, and answer all the questions that would be coming in from all those agents who didn't have any problems—the great majority, I might add—and are now wondering what all the commotion is about. I think the responsible business decision to make right now is to say that we made a mistake and we're going to have to live with it.

A notice went out to all agents apprising them that EGI was aware of the problem but that under the circumstances nothing would be done about it until the next round of product/

pricing changes—probably a year from now. Balducci thought
that the problem had been put to bed. He was mistaken:

> Next Ed tells me that he got a call from one of our agents in
> Ohio—the same agent who called in the first place—and he wants
> to know if he can tear up a customer's policy and then rewrite
> another policy for that customer right on the spot. Apparently the
> pricing structure for *new* customers didn't have the same glitch that
> was there for existing customers. So this agent tells his customer:
> "We can take the old policy and cancel it. Then we'll treat you like
> a new customer. And you can get the lower price." I don't like
> the idea of playing games with the system like that, but the thing
> is, he already told the customer about it, so I'm not sure we can
> do anything but go along.
>
> You know, it's all well and good for agents to say things like that
> to customers: "All we have to do is tear up the old policy! No
> problem!" Yeah—no problem for them. But then we've got to fig-
> ure out a way to handle those cases back here—Sheila and the
> other programmers have to set up a system to deal with those
> cases. But that's the stuff that really gets me p.o.'d: "No problem!"
> Amazing how generous other people can be with the time of *my*
> people.

Sheila assured Balducci that setting up a system to handle
those "cancel/re-sign" cases really wasn't a very big deal after
all. Basically, it would involve making sure that the field agents
attached a note to each new application indicating that it was,
in fact, a case of cancel/re-sign and including the old account
number for cross-referencing. Of course, that in turn meant
that instructions had to go out to the field agents through Ed's
marketing support department. Three weeks later, the results
of their efforts appeared to be in. Balducci sums it up:

> "We have a major problem!" "How can you screw things up that
> way!" "Why are you jerking my customers around like that!" That's
> the sort of thing we hear all the time from the field. You know,
> "The sky is falling!" That's what we heard with this minor pricing
> problem. So what happens? One agent gets the idea to cancel
> policies and then re-sign them. He tells the customer that that's "a
> possibility." Of course, after he said that, he tells me, "But I already
> told the customer!" I don't like having a gun held to my head like

that. But we do what's right. We set up a system to handle those cases. We get word out to the field agents. We handle their phone calls. All that stuff gets done by people who already don't have time to do what they should be spending their time doing. But we do it. And do you know what happens? Nobody cares! Do you know how many customers took advantage of this slick new system we set up to handle *all* those cases? Two. The guy who called in the first place, and one other person. Probably his cousin. The sky is falling, my ass. It fell about an inch and a quarter. All of that time and effort to deal with two cases. It makes you wonder: Don't people understand how much work is involved?

✳ ✳ ✳

What was the defect in the product/service offered by EGI?

There was a palpable mistake in the pricing structure for the insurance rates. Obviously, had that not happened in the first place, or had the error been caught before the material was sent out to customers, EGI's problems could have been avoided. Any techniques that reduce the number of such "product defects" will serve to improve quality.

What was the defect in the transaction?

The bureaucratic response given by EGI to the customer (through the Ohio agent).

What was the source of this transaction defect?

A failure on the part of Balducci's people to understand their role in the total transaction. They did not seem to understand the "connectedness" between their work and the customer. They viewed things in terms of how much work would be involved rather than focusing on why they were doing that work in the first place (i.e., to serve customers). They also tended to see things as static rather than dynamic. From Balducci's point of view, the defect was in the pricing structure. He didn't seem to realize that even though the pricing documentation seemed to be "fixed" in time, the transaction was still very much alive, and that customers would be "keeping score" throughout the whole, dynamic process.

More than likely, what was the Ohio customer's initial reaction when he noticed the illogic of EGI's pricing structure?

He was probably confused, puzzled—maybe moderately annoyed. But chances are he was not all that upset and was probably still more than willing to listen to reason.

By the end of this entire scenario, what was the Ohio customer's likely attitude?

"What the hell are those lousy SOB's at EGI trying to pull?" Or words to that effect.

Why?

Because customers are willing to make allowances for mistakes made in good faith. They understand that "these things happen" and intuitively make allowances for that fact in their perceptions of overall transaction quality. What customers will not tolerate or accept is the kind of bureaucratic "the system is what the system is and there's nothing that can be done about it" response that they got from EGI.

What did the Ohio agent do correctly?

He didn't blindly accept the fact that "nothing can be done" and sought out a resolution to his customer's problem.

How could the Ohio agent have handled the situation better?

The cancel/re-sign approach did effectively cope with the problem at hand, but it dealt with just the symptoms and not the root cause of the problem. The agent could have gone back to EGI and said something like: "I'm out here trying like hell to make us all some money. You send something out here that is wrong, customers notice that it's wrong, you admit that it's wrong, but then you say we're not going to do anything about it. Well, pardon me for saying so, but that's a crock. We're asking people for serious money to deal with serious matters—medical care. If you want me to stop 'playing games with the system,' as you put it, then stop treating the system like it's just a goddam game. It's not. This is real life. We're dealing with real people, with real problems. And real people tend to have a rather low tolerance for that type of crap!"

What was EGI's reaction to the agent who flagged the problem?

At best, forbearance, although annoyance would probably come closer to describing it.

What should the reaction have been?

"Thanks for complaining!"

What functions could be said to have responsibility for the transaction process defect?

- Whoever was responsible for ensuring that the pricing structure was internally consistent. Probably marketing.
- Balducci, for offering up such a vast array of dumb responses to the situation at hand.
- Marketing support (Ed), programming (Sheila), the field sales force (the Ohio agent), and everyone else who let Balducci get away with offering such dumb responses.
- The human resources/organizational development functions for not ensuring that all functions understood their fundamental connectedness to the customer and taking the steps necessary to make that happen.
- Top management, for fostering attitudes and creating a climate in which all of the above could happen.

What are the costs of unquality for EGI in this scenario?

- The time and effort spent in fielding agents' questions.
- The time and effort spent in deciding on "what to do."
- The time and effort spent in setting up the cancel/re-sign system.
- Hassle for EGI's customers.
- Hassle for EGI's agents.
- Being made to look foolish in the eyes of customers and agents.
- Reinforcement of a "good enough" attitude throughout Balducci's organization.
- Reinforcement of a "don't they know how much work is involved" attitude throughout Balducci's organization.
- Loss of customers—customers who canceled their EGI policies but *didn't* re-sign (which could account for the fact that only two people used the ad hoc cancel/re-sign system).
- Loss of goodwill—customers who didn't cancel but who were left with a bad taste in their mouths by the whole situation.

What can Wayne Balducci do to make sure that similar situations don't occur in the future?

- Adopt a "transaction quality" mind set.
- Recognize that everyone has a part to play in the process of delivering quality transactions.
- Make sure that everyone in the organization adopts the same mind set.

Ask Mr. Quality!

Dear Mr. Quality:

I am a telephone sales representative for a major New York publishing company. This week I received a call from a customer who asked if I could get her order for two books (big spender!) in just three days' time! Don't these people understand that this is our busy season? To top things off, it turned out that she was not even a regular customer; it would have taken at least three days to get her credit approved!

I told her that I would do the best I could, and that got her off the line. But now I'm worried that she might call up again with a similarly unreasonable request and I'll have to go through the whole process again. Can you give me some advice on how to put an end to such nuisance calls once and for all?

Loretta Selavy

PANDER PUBLISHING
WHITE PLAINS, NEW YORK

Dear Ms. Selavy:

If your objective is to stop getting "nuisance calls" from Customers, then Mr. Quality doesn't think you need any advice from him. You're doing just fine. May Mr. Quality be so bold as to suggest that you use the time that would otherwise have been wasted with such calls in preparing for your imminent career move out of the selling profession?

Dear Mr. Quality:

I'm a property manager for a major hotel chain, and I'm sure you know what a tough job that is. I mean, the way some people act as though they're doing you this huge favor by staying at your hotel and all! Anyway, about three years ago, we came up with what I thought was a real good idea. To keep guests from helping themselves to those nice wooden clothes hangers we provide for them—those aren't cheap, you know—we started using the ones without hooks. You know what I'm talking about—the ones that stay attached to the bar in the closet. "Pinhead hangers," we call them. Well, last week I got a call from Housekeeping. Somebody had stolen one of the pinhead hangers and left a note in its place. The note said: "In protest!" I'm confused. Those hangers aren't any good to anybody but us! Any ideas about what that note was supposed to mean?

Kotler F. Douglas

PROPERTY MANAGER
SANCTUARY INNS, "SANCTUARY'S THE NAME, GRACIOUSNESS THE GAME"
WOOK, IOWA

Dear Mr. Douglas:

Mr. Quality hasn't a clue as to what that delightfully mischievous and altogether justified note might mean, but he does think it nicely appropriate that you are so well-versed in the use of pinhead hangers.

Dear Mr. Quality:

Do you know what really galls me? When my customers can't figure out how to read my bill and wind up sending me the wrong amount. But, then, I guess if they could add their way out of a paper bag, they wouldn't need me.

W. Wendell Wendell

CERTIFIED PUBLIC ACCOUNTANT
PERTH-BY-THE-BAY, OKLAHOMA

Dear Mr. Wendell:

And your question is?

Dear Mr. Quality:

I spend my entire professional life dealing with what I consider to be a perverse feature of an otherwise reasonably well-ordered universe. Why is it that we must spend months upon months doing market segmentation studies, profiling the customers who populate each of the segments, analyzing the cost-benefit trade-offs of each increment of applied technology added to our products, defining product specifications, determining price elasticity behavior, developing distribution channels, training the sales force, and launching advertising, promotional, and PR campaigns only to find out that, by the time we get the product to market, the premises on which the initial segmentation studies were made have been rendered invalid by fickle customer behavior?

Eileen McNamara

VICE PRESIDENT, STRATEGIC MARKETING
BIG ED'S BUSINESS SOFTWARE AND CLAM BAR
EYEGOTMYNE, CALIFORNIA

Dear Ms. McNamara:

First of all, Mr. Quality couldn't help but be impressed by the exceptional level of grace and modesty displayed in your letter—a level far beyond that customarily expected from vice-presidents of strategic marketing. Mr. Quality, too, considers the universe to be "reasonably well-ordered" and is gratified to have had that opinion validated.

As to the substantive point you raised: As it happens, it is one to which Mr. Quality has given not inconsiderable thought over the years. It is true that Customers' wants, needs, opinions, and fancies are prone to flit around in waterbug fashion. It is also true that attempting to discern those wants, meet those needs, address those opinions, and strike those fancies is a sometimes daunting task, giving rise to things like peptic ulcers, strategic marketing departments, and the near criminal syndication fees commanded these days by Mr. Quality's advice column.

A possible resolution to this conundrum was presented to Mr. Quality recently while he was watching a professional football game. (Yes: a guilty pleasure confessed to!) On this particular Sunday, Mr. Quality had the Vikings plus, as it were, three against the Raiders. Alas, a length-of-the-field drive in the game's final thirty-seven seconds gave the Raiders a four-point win. After clearing away the debris in his living room resulting from a jalopeña-bean-dip-can-induced implosion of a Trinitron picture tube, Mr. Quality reflected on what, as fate would have it, turns out to be your conundrum, Ms. McNamara. How had the Raiders been able to move eighty-eight yards before thirty-seven seconds had elapsed on the game clock? With Marc Wilson at quarterback, no less?!?

Judicious use of their allotment of time-outs was the answer. Why, Mr. Quality mused, couldn't the Securities and Exchange Commission issue each publicly traded company an allotment of time-outs? Then, when faced with a situation such as the one so eloquently described in your letter, a company could simply "call a time-out," during which all activity in the relevant marketplace would cease, with the necessary policing to be done by SEC minions.

Or maybe not. It was just a thought.

Dear Mr. Quality:

Why is it that the magazines in doctors' offices are always six months old?

Mrs. Clark Griswold

CHICAGO, ILLINOIS

Dear Mrs. Griswold:

Depending on the sense of your question (it is, you will admit, ambiguous on this point), there are two possible answers. If you're puzzled as to why the magazines are so *old,* then it could be that they were new when you arrived for your appointment and you just didn't notice. If your observation is that they seem to be relatively *newer* than they used to be, the explanation is that a recent American Medical Association ruling requires that after six months they be resold to dentists.

Dear Mr. Quality:

I know that quality is a process-related issue, and I'm concerned about the process by which we elect our nation's presidents and the quality of the presidents who emerge from that process. Basically, I think the problem is that the process is much too long and drawn out. It becomes too forced. Staged. Artificial. Candidates don't have enough to say and reporters don't have enough to report to fill up the time, but that doesn't stop them from saying and reporting anyway. So I was thinking: Suppose, instead of being held in November, elections were held in the summer. (On the Fourth of July, perhaps?!?) That would knock four months off the election year right there. Plus which, since we still won't have switched back off daylight-savings time by

Election Day, we'd pick up another hour to boot. Then, instead of holding elections on the first Tuesday after the first Monday, we could have them on the first Monday after the first Sunday. There's another day cut off—and we could give people a three-day weekend in the process. That's not all. As things stand now, presidential elections are always held in leap years. Move it up or back a year and bingo—you lose another day. Not to mention that people won't be distracted by the Olympics any more.

So the way I figure it, just implementing these simple ideas would leave us with four months, two days, and one hour less for candidates and reporters to say and do silly things. What do you think?

G. R. Ford

VAIL, COLORADO

Dear Mr. Ford:

Mr. Quality finds your ideas to be most interesting and would like more time to explore all facets of the wholly worthwhile issues you raise before commenting further.

Dear Mr. Quality:

Two months ago, I was laid off from my job as director of industrial engineering for a division of a Fortune 500 company. I've been diligently looking for work ever since, but so far I've had no luck. As a result, I've been spending upwards of an hour each week standing in line to collect my unemployment compensation check. I should say, I've been standing in lines, plural! First, you stand in a line to get your ID number verified. Then you stand in another line to sign a form. Then it's off to a third line to get your check. Honestly, the way things are set up in there has got to be the most illogical, inefficient, unproductive process imaginable. Why must it be so?

Maura Mildew

COLUMBUS, OHIO

Dear Ms. Mildew:

But if there were only one line instead of three, the people who now service those lines would be (1) unemployed, and therefore (2) in them. The one remaining line would be that much longer and the total time you would have to spend in that line would be (Mr. Quality asks you to trust him on this) the same. So you see, it is logical after all.

The Whole,
The Sum of the Parts, Etc.

"Just who is it," they asked, "for whom
    The line of responsibility's clean?"
"Why don't *you* tell *me?*" the quality guru replied,
    guruishly serene.

"Well, marketing defines it,
    so we have a role to play."
"But engineering designs it.
    Least that's what I say."
"Won't be nothing to define or design
    unless of course finance funds it."
"An assembly line's gotta go to work and
    manufacturing runs it."
"That line will rust or flood or be blown away without
    appropriate facilities."
"But it's HR that provides the resources
    with appropriate human abilities."
"Sales must sell on quality. We've gotta
    offer people 'the best.' "
"Sales might sell the first one, but it's
    service that sells the rest."
"If accounting shuts down, bills and checks don't go out,
    and nobody pays—or gets paid."
"Keep the paperwork flowing, the process going,
    that's administration's crusade."

The guru thought, "Though they might disagree, they share
    a gloriously indisputable passion."
So he figured he owed them a quality response
    in guruishly inscrutable fashion.

He stopped and he looked and he smiled then he paused,
    lips pursed, semiscrutably tight.
"Each of you is wrong, alas.
        But all of you are right."

6

The Hidden Opportunities

I have defined quality as "that which meets the customer's expectations." But is *meeting* the customer's expectations enough? Doesn't quality really have to do with *exceeding* those expectations? As usual, my answer is a solid, categorical: "Sort of." (I mentioned that my background was in marketing; old habits are hard to break.) The objective of striving for quality is—or ought to be—ensuring that your customers feel (and that's exactly the right word) that your organization is a *special* one with which to do business. Certainly, if you regularly exceed customers' expectations, they will have a very strong sense of perceived quality. But quality, as I've also said, can't be viewed as some sort of puffy abstraction. If you're going to achieve it, then that "it" had better be clear, clean, and bounded. Meeting customer expectations provides that sort of explicit target. A general notion of exceeding expectations would seem to let the genie back out of the bottle. How to reconcile the apparent contradictions?

Consider a hypothetical transaction. You go to a department store and purchase a snazzy new piece of consumer electronics—say, a compact disk player. You bring it home, unpack it, plug it in, turn it on—and nothing happens. It doesn't work. Yes, you read the instructions carefully and followed them exactly. No, it was not a case of "pilot error" (which I once heard described by a *marketing* person as "the nut behind the wheel"). Clearly, there is a product quality problem.

But as noted quality guru Yogi Berra so insightfully put it, "It ain't over till it's over." Although the product defect has already occurred, the transaction itself is still very much alive. In fact, it's more alive than *ever* in your mind, since you had expected to spend the evening listening to music and not trying to figure out how and when you're going to get the defective CD player back to a department store that's twelve miles away, and this is an impossibly busy week for you, and, besides, why should you have to go through this hassle in the first place? The money you gave the department store works just fine, unlike the overpriced paper weight you were sold!

I think it's safe to say that the way the department store handles things from here on out will have a lot to do with your overall sense of "what it's like to do business with those people." What would it take for the store to deliver quality throughout the rest of the transaction? What are your expectations for how the situation ought to be handled?

First and foremost, it shouldn't cost another nickel out of your pocket. In effect you've already given the store a loan (interest-free, no less) and have no real desire to stay in the banking business any longer than you have to.

Second, you would expect a replacement CD player more or less immediately. If the store were to say, "You'll have to send the unit you bought to the factory for repairs. It's all covered under the warranty, so it won't cost you anything," you'd probably be inclined to respond, "Stuff and nonsense." (I would probably be inclined to respond more strongly.) You would expect the store to take the bad one back and give you a new (i.e., different) one. Now.

Third, the remainder of the transaction should be hassle-free. The fact that you have to take the damn thing back to the store is hassle enough: "OK, the thing doesn't work. I suppose those things happen. I don't want to have to make another trip to the store. I guess I have to. But people sure as hell better not hassle me about it when I get there." And, as it happens, you'd be right; they sure as hell better not.

Fourth, you would expect simple, common courtesy. Empathy might be better, but courtesy will do. Pretty basic, I know, but nonetheless important.

So if, when you went back to the store, you got a replacement CD player with no hassles and at no extra cost, and you were treated courteously along the way, your expectations would be met. The remainder of the transaction would be defect-free; it would be a quality transaction.

A reasonable enough conclusion to draw. But now I'd like you to consider another example, this one real, not hypothetical. What follows is an excerpt from an article in the July 30, 1985 issue of the *Wall Street Journal;* it tells of an experience that the writer and her husband had with the Odakyu Department Store in Tokyo. While you're reading this, keep in mind the notions of "customer expectations" and "transaction quality":

Japan's Got Us Beat in the Service Department, Too

BY HILARY HINDS KITASEI

My husband and I bought one souvenir the last time we were in Tokyo—a Sony compact disk player. The transaction took seven minutes at the Odakyu Department Store, including time to find the right department and to wait while the salesman filled out a second charge slip after misspelling my husband's name on the first.

My in-laws, who were our hosts in the outlying city of Sagamihara, were eager to see their son's purchase, so he opened the box for them the next morning. But when he tried to demonstrate the player, it wouldn't work. We peered inside. It had no innards! My husband used the time until the Odakyu would open at 10 to practice for the rare opportunity in that country to wax indignant. But at a minute to 10 he was preempted by the store ringing us.

My mother-in-law took the call, and had to hold the receiver away from her ear against the barrage of Japanese honorifics. Odakyu's vice president was on his way over with a new disk player.

A taxi pulled up 50 minutes later and spilled out the vice president and a junior employee who was laden with packages and a clipboard. In the entrance hall the two men bowed vigorously.

The younger man was still bobbing as he read from a log that recorded the progress of their efforts to rectify their mistake, beginning at 4:32 P.M. the day before, when the salesclerk alerted the store's security guards to stop my husband at the door. When that didn't work, the clerk turned to his supervisor, who turned to his supervisor, until a SWAT team leading all the way to the vice president was in place to work on the only clues, a name and an American Express card number. Remembering that the customer had asked him about using the disk player in the U.S., the clerk called 32 hotels in and around Tokyo to ask if a Mr. Kitasel was registered. When that turned up nothing, the Odakyu commandeered a staff member to stay until 9 P.M. to call American Express headquarters in New York. American Express gave him our New York telephone number. It was after 11 when he reached my parents, who were staying at our apartment. My mother gave him my in-laws' telephone number.

The younger man looked up from his clipboard and gave us, in addition to the new $280 disk player, a set of towels, a box of cakes, and a Chopin disk. Three minutes after this exhausted pair had arrived they were climbing back into the waiting cab. The vice president suddenly dashed back. He had forgotten to apologize for my husband having to wait while the salesman had rewritten the charge slip, but he hoped we understood that it had been the young man's first day.*

Now consider the following questions:

Which transaction was "better"—the one in the hypothetical example or the one at the Odakyu? I think it's safe to say that the majority of people would unhesitatingly answer: "The Odakyu." And I would agree.

Now to the trick question. Which transaction was of "higher

---

quality"? Again, I would expect the answer to come back at roughly the same percentage: "The Odakyu." But here I would disagree.

Quality is "that which meets the customer's expectations." In the case of a defective compact disk player, those expectations are no additional out-of-pocket cost, prompt replacement, no hassles, common courtesy. If a department store meets those expectations, has it delivered quality? Yes. If a store exceeds those expectations, as the Odakyu did, has it delivered quality? Yes. Understand, the Odakyu has clearly delivered *more* of *something*. The question becomes: Just what is the "it" that the Odakyu has delivered more of?

Is it more quality? Not according to the customer expectations definition. For that matter, not according to any of the standard, widely accepted definitions of quality, all of which share one fundamental premise: Quality is a yes/no proposition. You establish a requirement. If you conform to it, you have achieved quality. If you don't, you haven't. There are other ways to put it. Black and white. Either/or. Digital as opposed to analog. A step function vs. a continuum. But they all amount to the same thing. That being the case, it is imprecise to think in terms of higher or lower quality. The more precise distinction is between quality and *un*quality.

The fact is that *both* the hypothetical and the Odakyu transactions are quality transactions. The reality is that the Odakyu transaction is undeniably better. How do you reconcile those two statements? The answer, as usual, comes from looking at things from the customer's perspective.

When customers enter into transactions, what are they looking for? Certainly a very important part of what they're looking for is a product or service that will work and continue to work for a reasonable period of time—with the definition of "reasonable" determined by the relevant (macro)expectations in that marketplace. Customers are looking for a minimum of problems in the mechanics of carrying out that transaction. ZERO DEFECTS and HASSLE FREE might be the bumper sticker ways of putting it. Which, when you think about it, is a fair description of customer expectations in the hypothetical

CD example. Let me generalize and describe that category of customer objectives as the *absence of defects:* obviously reasonable and eminently important.

But is the absence of defects *all* that customers are looking for? Is it all that *you* look for as a customer? Is that the mind set you want your customers to have when they engage in transactions with you? As in: "My only hope is that you folks not screw this one up too badly." I don't know about you, but I don't think that's the optimum platform from which to be selling. The only way I know to *guarantee* (thereby setting expectations) that there will be a defect-free transaction is to have a *transaction-free* transaction, and I don't think that's the path you want to be going down. If the best the customer can hope for is a wash—the absence of anything negative—then why would a customer want to engage in a transaction in the first place?

The answer is that customers don't enter into transactions to avoid negatives; they do so to receive something positive. When I get up in the morning, I fully expect that I won't be hit by a bus that day. Call me a cockeyed optimist, but it's an expectation that has been fulfilled every day now for almost forty years. At night, though, when I mentally run through a quick assessment of the day's events, I don't say: "Well, I wasn't hit by a bus. What more could I have hoped for?" Quite a lot actually, and the same holds true for your customers. Of course they want the absence of defects. They don't want to be "hit by a bus" either. But they're also looking for the presence of something positive.

In both the hypothetical and the Odakyu cases, the defects were removed. But the Odakyu took things further than that. For one thing, the store lowered the cost to the customer. How?

1. By tracking down the customer and calling him, thereby minimizing the amount of time that the customer had to ask himself: "I wonder how I'm going to clear this situation up?"
2. By delivering the replacement CD player to the custom-

er's house, thereby saving the customer time, hassle, and the out-of-pocket costs associated with returning to the store.

3. By dramatically lowering the cost of lost confidence in the supplier that occurs whenever a transaction "breaks."

On the last point, I'm not talking about the cost to the supplier's reputation; that's certainly related, but not of interest here. I'm talking about the fact that the degree of confidence that a customer has in a supplier is a very real asset to that customer. It translates directly into things like how much time the customer must devote to deciding where to go to buy "the next one," how much energy the customer must put into monitoring (read: worrying about) the current transaction, and so on. A broken transaction chips away at supplier confidence, and that's a very real cost to the customer. The obvious and substantial level of concern and effort shown by the Odakyu reduced that cost to the customer.

In fact, not only did the Odakyu enable the customer to recover the confidence that might have been lost. The transaction was handled so well that the store, net, *added* to the customer's level of confidence.

So when you sum it all up, what did the Odakyu do that was different? It lowered the cost while delivering more. It's interesting to look at that as a ratio:

$$\frac{\text{What the customer } \textbf{got}}{\text{What it } \textbf{cost} \text{ the customer}} \quad = \quad ???$$

There is a word for that ratio of got to cost, and that word is "value." That's the positive thing that customers are looking for: *value.* And that's true for any business, any customer, any product, any service, any time, anywhere.

- *Quality* is what you must manage.
- *Value* is what your customers feel.

And since the reason for paying attention to quality in the first place is to ensure that your customers feel that you are a *special* organization with which to do business, then your quality efforts ought to be focused on ensuring, not just the "absence of defects," but rather the "presence of value."

Just so there's no confusion on a rather key point: I'm not saying that you don't have to worry about the absence of defects. Obviously you do. Focusing on delivering value leaves you no choice but to eliminate defects. The numerator in the ratio that defines value is "what the customer got." If the customer didn't eventually "get" a CD player with some working parts in it, clearly the quality of the transaction would not have been there. And since customers will very quickly cease to be charmed by bowing and scraping and cakes and towels, it behooves you to do whatever you can to see to it that defects do not occur in the first place. You've gotta deliver the goods.

But there is a difference in mind set between striving for the absence of defects and striving for the presence of value. Absence of defects is an obviously critical subset of presence of value. But it's that "presence of value" mind set that will get your organization to do those extra (read: different) things, like calling thirty-two hotels and conducting a worldwide search for the customer who purchased the hollow CD player. And that in turn is what will make you stand out from the crowd and get articles written about you in the *Wall Street Journal*.

The accompanying diagram illustrates the relevant differences between the hypothetical handling of the hollow CD player and the way the Odakyu Department Store handled it. Below the dashed line are all the things that must be done in order to *meet* customer expectations. Above the dashed line are the things done by the Odakyu that *exceeded* expectations. The dashed line represents "quality," the point where expectations are met. If you're at or over the line, you've achieved quality. If you're under the line, you haven't. Period. The Odakyu transaction was better than the hypothetical transaction—not "of higher quality," but "better"—because it delivered more value, it had a higher got/cost ratio. That's what the customer perceives. That's what the customer feels. That's what the customer acts upon: the presence of value and not just the absence of defects.

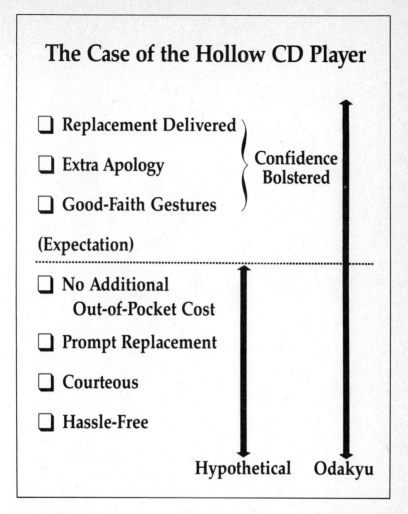

The Case of the Hollow CD Player

❏ Replacement Delivered ⎫
❏ Extra Apology ⎬ **Confidence Bolstered**
❏ Good-Faith Gestures ⎭

(Expectation)

❏ No Additional Out-of-Pocket Cost

❏ Prompt Replacement

❏ Courteous

❏ Hassle-Free

Hypothetical   Odakyu

It's in that sense that quality—the absence of defects, conformance to requirements, meeting customer expectations: call it what you will—can be thought of as *minimum acceptable value.* The key word is "mimimum." Achieving it doesn't win the game for you; it merely allows you to keep playing. The simple distribution curve displayed on page 142 illustrates how the various players in a market tend to sort out relative to the "value delivered." Some will exceed expectations, some will fall below expectations, and the majority will cluster around

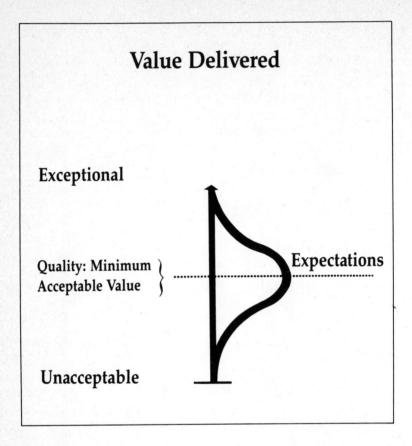

Value Delivered

Exceptional

Quality: Minimum
Acceptable Value

Expectations

Unacceptable

expectations. That should come as no surprise at all. How do expectations (and here I'm talking about macroexpectations: the standard industry practice of the day) get set? By a summing of what *most* people experience in dealing with *most* organizations *most* of the time.

By "exceeding expectations" you can gain a near-term selling advantage. Consider what the Odakyu is effectively offering its customers: "If you buy a defective product at one of our competitors' stores, you will have to bring it in yourself to get a replacement. If—God forbid!—you buy it at the Odakyu, we will deliver a replacement to you. And we might even throw in some cakes and towels for good measure."

But the situation isn't static; it's dynamic. As competitors realize that they are losing business because of the value differential, they will begin matching the Odakyu's offering. It's not that everybody will become exceptional; that would be a logical impossibility. Rather, expectations will move higher and pull with them the level of mimimum acceptable value—the "quality" point. As the differential narrows, the Odakyu's near-term selling advantage will be mitigated somewhat. But the store will retain the long-term strategic advantage of being perceived as leading the way when it comes to providing transaction value.

And that's where the real payoff—the hidden opportunity—of quality resides. In the real world, which brings with it change and competitive pressure, no position is permanently safe. That's not the way it works. But if you can attain a position where your competition is reacting to you, where you're defining the agenda—well, that's an awfully nice position to be in. And it comes from a difference in mind set. It's the difference between looking at quality as the ending point, in which case you will constantly be chasing expectations, or looking at quality as the starting point, in which case you will be the one setting and resetting expectations. It's the difference between "planning not to fail" and "planning to succeed." It's a difference that is large.

When I told the Odakyu story during a seminar on customer satisfaction, one participant raised his hand and observed: "The Odakyu probably sells that hollow CD player to somebody different every day. That's the only job that that vice-president and his assistant have. They're in charge of the cakes and towels." Everybody laughed, and I joked about how shocked I was that we've become so cynical. (For the record, I don't for a minute think that that's really what happened.) But it is an interesting observation. Because it begins to suggest the opportunity that exists to add value, exceed expectations throughout the entire transaction, and gain a competitive advantage in the process.

And you don't have to wait for defects to occur. Finding ways to add value relative to customer expectations at any point of contact throughout the transaction will have the same effect. All the same, there are several reasons for focusing here on a defective transaction. First of all, organizations tend to think of quality in terms of defects: identifying them, correcting them, and eliminating their causes. Second, a defective transaction shows a more clear-cut need. You avoid the "if it ain't broke don't fix it" objection. Third, and perhaps most interesting of all, a defective transaction is precisely the moment at which business organizations have the greatest opportunity to stand out in their customers' eyes.

It's ironic when you think about it, but organizations will spend millions of dollars on advertising and promotion, at least one objective of which is "to get people's attention." Well, if there's one thing you can be sure of, it's that when a defect occurs in a transaction you have the customer's attention. At that moment the customer is keenly aware of and sharply focused on what it means to do business with you. You *will* stand out in the customer's eyes; on that point you have no choice. The choice you do have is whether to stand out for being unacceptable or for being exceptional.

Thinking in terms of value also helps you get around some of the knee-jerk "quality costs too much" reactions you're apt to run up against, because cost is factored into the value ratio. *By definition*, value means "at an acceptable cost." If whatever action step you decide to take costs the customer too much, then it's not of value, and the marketplace will tell you so. You can't simply say: "Sure we could do a lot better and deliver extra value if we could just hire twenty-six more people." That might increase the "what the customer got"; but it might also increase the "cost to the customer"—those twenty-six people aren't, presumably, working for free—by a proportionally greater amount. Result? Value down, not up. "Well," comes the response, "it's hard to figure out ways to deliver more to customers without canceling it out in higher costs." To which there is a two-part answer: (1) that's why they call it work, and why it's hard to be the best; and (2) before you can be the best, you have to be better, unless of course you already are the best, in which case you can *still* be better and solidify your leadership position.

Another not uncommon lament: "We could provide higher quality, but our customers just don't want to pay for it." (Note: Whenever you hear a comparative modify "quality," warning bells ought to sound in your head.) One possible explanation is that the added increment in product or service really would be worthwhile, and the customer just doesn't realize it. But whose responsibility is it to see that the customer understands how worthwhile it really is? Isn't the effective communication of product benefits part of the transaction you want the customer to buy? To the extent that you haven't effectively communicated that added benefit, a degree of unquality exists in the transaction.

A second explanation is that your customers fully understand and realize exactly what the added increment is all about and simply do not want it. They don't perceive that they are getting anything (or enough) extra to justify the added cost. In other words, the value isn't there for them. In still other words, there isn't a market for the product you'd *like* to deliver. That's a painful realization, and it explains why it's tempting to assume a self-righteous "we could deliver more quality but our customers just don't understand" stance. Focusing on value can help you avoid this sort of deadly pearls-before-swine attitude.

Shifting the focus from the "absence of defects" to the "presence of value" does not mean you have to be any less rigorous or single-minded about quality. You're not letting the genie back out of the bottle. With either approach you have to have a crystal-clear understanding of what customer expectations are (i.e., what quality is) and how you stack up against them. The only question is whether you view quality as a ceiling or as the foundation on which you can build significant competitive advantage.

To see how that works, let's revisit the "Jerry the paperboy" example presented in the last chapter. Pretty much everything in that discussion flowed from an "absence of defects" objective and mentality (i.e., focusing "below the line" in the figure on page 142). Jerry needed to make sure that the papers were delivered on time and on the right days. He had to be certain they were always left at the same place, and not at the front door one day, the back door the next. Or worse, in a mud puddle one day, on the roof the next. He needed to be sure that there were no mistakes in his recordkeeping. That when he went away, he had reliable substitutes who would get the papers out and not foul up his relationships with his customers. And so on.

If Jerry were to do all these "below the line" things, he would deliver a quality transaction. His customers would perceive quality. Now, "the old Jerry" (if such an expression makes any sense with a twelve-year-old) would have stopped there: "I will meet those expectations, deliver quality, and have achieved my goal." "The new Jerry" looks at things differently. He understands what those expectations are and realizes that he must do whatever it takes to meet them. But he sees them as merely the *starting* point. He sees quality as minimum acceptable value. And he looks for ways to build on that foundation of quality by adding even more value (i.e., he looks for things that can be done "above the line" in the figure on page 142).

Now when Jerry signs up new customers, he doesn't just drop the paper on their front step on the first day of delivery. He makes a point of stopping by, introducing himself, and thanking them for their business. (Has that ever happened to you? Me neither.)

Jerry makes sure the new customers have his name and a phone number to call "just in case you have any questions or need to reach me." (The customers will probably never have to use the number, but it's nice to have it.) The implicit message from Jerry is: "I'm not afraid to be held accountable." And that gives his customers added confidence in him.

Jerry also asks new customers where the paper should be left. (Leaving the paper in the right place may not be any different; *asking* is.)

When customers call to tell Jerry they'll be going on vacation (which Jerry made easier for them by leaving his name and number), he comes by and takes two minutes of their time to fill out a form documenting when they'd like delivery stopped and restarted and what they'd like him to do with the papers over that period. (Have you ever called a paperboy with that sort of message? Or shouted it to him one morning as he pedaled off after making a delivery? How confident were you that he really got the message? Wouldn't Jerry's approach make you feel better? Add confidence? Add value for you in the transaction?)

When it's time for Jerry and his family to go on vacation, he takes his substitute carrier around the entire route, introduces her to his customers, gives the customers the substitute's name and phone number, and makes sure the customers know when he'll be back from vacation. (How many paperboys do this? Isn't that the whole point—striving for positive differentiators?)

While all this is going on, of course, there had still better be an absence of defects. It's nice for Jerry to provide all these extra touches, but they're extra only if he's also doing the baseline stuff. An introduction to the vacation substitute won't make up for late or soggy papers. Nor should it. First and foremost, Jerry's gotta deliver the goods. He's gotta deliver a quality transaction. And if he does that, his customers won't cancel their subscriptions and buy their papers at a convenience store instead. He gets to stay in the game.

But by viewing that as just a starting point and constantly looking for ways to add even more value throughout the transaction, Jerry will wind up with happier customers and good word of mouth, which in turn will lead to customers who are both more plentiful and more loyal. Not only will Jerry ensure that customers have no reason to leave him (the absence of negatives); he will be giving them reasons to stay (the presence of positives). And—this *is* a business after all, not a charity—he will get bigger tips, which as everybody knows is where you make the real money with a paper route.

It all comes down to a few simple factors:

Customers have the money.

You want it.

They decide who gets it.

They make those decisions *at the margin*. The question that they are implicitly asking every time they mull over a purchase decision (or a buy/bye decision) is: "Where can I get the most for my money?" In other words, got/cost. In other words, value.

Whatever your business enterprise is, you will do a better job of ensuring that the answer comes out in your favor if you view things from the perspective of the customer and follow the same line of reasoning Jerry followed:

- Quality is that which meets the customer's expectations.
- Quality means transaction quality, not just product or service quality.
- Quality is a starting point not an ending point, with a focus on the presence of value and not the absence of defects.

That's how to reconcile the need to manage quality (thereby hitting expectations) with the fact that customers gravitate toward the supplier who exceeds their expectations. Work from these premises and you'll be the one with a near-term selling advantage and long-term strategic advantage. All from understanding and then building on the true nature of quality— as felt by the customer.

Some *Positive* Real-Life Examples As Told by Some Real-Life Customers

Here are ten real-life examples of how customers perceive the presence of value and the effect that it has on them. The stories represent a broad range of businesses, and they are all told in the words of the customers themselves. In some cases, although the transaction described was in some way defective, taking a "presence of value" approach enabled the supplier organization not only to neutralize the potential damage but also to turn the situation to its advantage. In other cases, the supplier organization sought out ways to add value without being prompted by any transaction defects, seeing any point of contact with a customer as an opportunity to differentiate itself.

In all cases, the supplier's actions led customers to respond positively to the following types of questions about their experience:

- Would you be more inclined to buy the product or service?
- To stay with this supplier?
- To pass on good "word of mouth" about your experience?
- To have a strong sense that there's something different, something *special* about "doing business with those people"?

In all cases, the stories are intended to leave you asking the question: "How can the organization *I'm* a part of make *our customers* feel that way?"

There is, I freely admit, a certain sameness to these stories, a certain "niceness" and "comfortableness." But that's part of the point. Occasionally, you may find yourself in situations where adjectives like "dramatic" and "spectacular" apply, and that's fine. But as a day-in, day-out proposition, nice and comfortable are what customers value. Nice and comfortable, sad to say, *are* special. And you know they're special, because you can identify with what it's like to be the customer and how you would feel if you found yourself engaged in transactions like the following.

✳ ✳ ✳

I do a lot of business traveling. I'm on airplanes all the time. The whole routine is sort of second nature to me. You get to the airport, check in, sit around the departure gate, board the plane, take off, have a cup of coffee, try to get some work done, "return your seatback and tray table to the full upright and locked position," land, get off the plane, and go about your business. After a while you get kind of numbed by the whole ordeal. It's a good thing you become numbed; I think it's what helps you keep your sanity.

Well, last week I was getting off a plane in Atlanta, walking down the ramp—you know, that jetway thing—and as I got to the terminal I happened to glance up, and I noticed that over the door was an electronic message board that said something like, "Baggage for this flight can be picked up at Baggage Claim Area B." And that really got me! Maybe other airlines do that, but I'd never seen it before. I thought, "That's pretty neat. You don't have to go through that needle-in-a-haystack business of trying to figure out where your bags are." Now, I hadn't even checked any baggage. Almost never do. But it really made an impression on me that that airline was all right.

Then about a month later I was in the Orlando airport. You know, the one where everybody is wearing mouse ears. Anyway, I'm at the monitor that tells me when my flight is scheduled to leave, and I notice that right next to it is a monitor giving information about the weather at the destinations for all of the airline's flights.

It was the same airline that had the baggage claim sign in Atlanta. I guess it figures.

❋ ❋ ❋

I had a 1:00 P.M. dentist appointment, which put a big hole in the middle of my day, but it was the only time I could get. At about 11:00 A.M. I get a phone call. It's the dentist's secretary. She tells me that the dentist had two emergency cases that morning and his schedule is all backed up. He asked her to call all of his appointments that day, explain the situation, let patients know that he was running at least two hours late, and give them the option of coming in anyway or moving their appointment to another day.

I was stunned. That was about the most courteous thing I'd ever heard of from a dentist. Now if only doctors would start doing business the same way we'd really be making progress.

❋ ❋ ❋

It was a brand-new house. We had been in it only about a week when we noticed that the kitchen floor was beginning to disintegrate. The grout between the tiles was cracking and chipping away, and once that happened the tiles themselves began to loosen.

Needless to say we weren't terribly pleased. This was our "dream house." We hadn't scrimped. We paid top dollar for the best builder in the area, the guy with the best reputation by far. And then the kitchen floor starts falling apart! We called the builder. He said he'd "take care of it." We weren't quite sure what that meant, but at that point we didn't have a lot of choice. He was the only game in town.

The next afternoon our house is turned upside down. The builder is there. The subcontractor who had put in the tile is there. The guy who sold the subcontractor the grout is there. All standing in the middle of our kitchen arguing about whose fault the problem was. The builder says that maybe the tile hasn't been installed properly. The tile guy says that it must have been a bad batch of grout. The grout salesman is bouncing up and down to show everybody that the floor has too much "give," implying that there is a structural problem with the house.

Needless to say, the confrontation got a little heated. There was probably three, four thousand dollars at stake here, and nobody was too eager to get stuck with it. I can't say as I blame any of them, but I also didn't care, just as long as we weren't the ones to get stuck.

Well, as things seemed about to come to a boil, the builder takes us aside and says, "Don't pay any attention to the arguing. It's all part of the game. I just want to make sure that you understand that no matter what happens, it won't cost you anything. It's my responsibility to get the problem fixed and to work things out with these guys. That's what you're paying me for."

It was at that moment that we realized why his reputation was so good. If we had had any residual doubts about whether he was worth the money, they vanished at that point. In a sense, we were glad the problem came up, because it gave us the reassurance we needed.

✳ ✳ ✳

All week long my three-year-old was excited about going to the circus. It was all he could talk about to anybody. Finally the big day arrives. As we're driving into the city he kept asking, "When are we gonna get to the circus?" I park the car, and he asks, "Is this the circus?" I had to tell him that no, this was a parking garage. We walk two blocks to the arena where the circus is. We get to the arena and start walking up the ramp to our seats. "Are we there yet?" The kid was practically coming out of his skin waiting to see the circus. I felt almost sorry for him, except for the fact that I also wanted to kill him because he was making me crazy.

Well, we get to our seats about two minutes before the circus begins. He's beaming, happy as can be. Then the lights go down, and the ringmaster's announcements blare out over the PA system—and my son lets out a howl and begins bawling. The darkness and the noise had scared him to death. All the clowns and the elephants and the acrobats start marching in and he's saying—shrieking: "I wanna go home!"

This went on for about ten minutes, and when he didn't get any better I decided to leave. But then an usher came up to us. He was an elderly gentleman. He told me later that he had taken on a part-time job at the arena after retiring.

Well, he had noticed that my son didn't seem to be enjoying the circus very much. Truth of the matter is that he would have had a hard time not noticing. He came up to me and asked if I'd mind if he talked to my son. I said, "Be my guest. But I'm not sure how happy he'll be to talk to a stranger." The usher nodded and held out his arms—and my son went right to him.

The usher sat down in the aisle, right next to me, with my son in his lap. And he just talked to him gently and told him about how his grandson had been a little bit upset by the circus but had come to like it a lot. It didn't happen all at once, but you could see that my son was listening and beginning to calm down. After about five minutes, he was back under control. After about ten minutes he seemed downright calm. And after fifteen minutes he was laughing and clapping and having a wonderful time. The usher gave him a hug and handed him back to me and then went back to his station at the foot of the aisle.

The punchline is that when we got home and my husband asked how we had enjoyed the circus, my son said that it was great—and that the best part was "the nice man in the red jacket." He wants to go back again next weekend. Probably to see his new friend. My husband is going to take him.

✳ ✳ ✳

One of our suppliers doesn't include a mailing address on its literature and stationery. Just a post office box number. Most of the time that's all we need—it's fine for regular business mail. But occasionally we have reason to send the supplier a package, and we might send it through a delivery service instead of the post office. Well, those delivery services don't know from post office boxes. They want a street address. So we have to call the supplier and ask for the street address each time. I know, I know—we could write it down somewhere. But we don't.

The last time I called I guess I let my annoyance show with the secretary I spoke to, because a minute after I hung up I got a call. It was from some accountant, I think. He wanted to know about the problem I had mentioned to the secretary. I told him about the mailing address business. He listened—didn't say much—and thanked me for my input.

I didn't think a whole lot about it, but about three months later, I got an invoice from that supplier and I noticed that the return address had both a box number and a street address. And wouldn't you know it, the next day I get a letter from that accountant thanking me for calling attention to the problem and telling me what the supplier had done to resolve it. You might expect that sort of thing from somebody in customer service, but from an *accountant?*

✳ ✳ ✳

My son gets a birthday present in the mail from my in-laws. He tears off the wrapping and I see the words SOME ASSEMBLY REQUIRED and right away I know I'm in trouble. It's one of those things with about a thousand parts, and the parts have that unique property of expanding when exposed to air. At least that's the only reason I can figure that you can never get all of them back in the box once you've taken them out.

It turns out that instead of the thousand parts it's supposed to have, this one comes with 998. Two are missing. Now you've got to get the picture clear in your mind. My in-laws live about 500 miles away, so it's not a simple matter of driving on over to the store where they bought it and clearing up the problem. Anyway, they have the sales slip. And since it was a gift, they had peeled off the price tag from the box. So I have no way of proving where it was bought, even though I know it was at a national chain and there's a local outlet just five minutes from my house. We could have shipped the thing back to my in-laws, but that would have been a hassle for them—and my son would have had to wait several more days for his present. We're talking about a seven-year-old kid here, so patience is not high on the list of words that you would use to describe him.

My wife says to call the local store and explain. I really don't have a lot of choice, and I don't relish making the call. I figure that I'm going to get a big runaround, have to jump through a lot of hoops. And I'm really not sure I would blame the store. We're talking about a seventy-five-dollar toy, and I couldn't really prove where it had been bought.

I call and explain the situation and the woman on the other end says: "No problem. Just bring it in and we'll give you another one."

Then she says, "Oh, wait a minute. Let me make sure we have another one in stock before you come over here for nothing." She puts me on hold for a minute. She comes back on and says that the toy is in stock. I pack the thing up as best I can and throw it into the car: I want to get there before the woman changes her mind or goes off duty. I get to the store and she has the replacement waiting for me. I was really impressed. The thing that impressed me the most was the fact that when I gave her the box with the missing parts, she never looked inside as if to say, "We're not sure that we trust you." I liked that.

✳ ✳ ✳

Right after I checked into my hotel room there was a knock at my door. It was the chambermaid asking if I wanted my bed turned down. I told her that I didn't. Then she handed me some matchbooks. I told her that I didn't smoke. She said that maybe I'd want to keep them as souvenirs. I thanked her and closed the door, but I couldn't imagine why she thought I'd want to keep the matches.

Then I looked at them. On one side was the name of the hotel. On the other side *my last name* was printed. I figured that either I had a cousin I didn't know about who ran a restaurant in the hotel or else the hotel extended this little gesture of hospitality to all its guests.

Nice touch. And I did save the matches to show to people.

✳ ✳ ✳

There's a lot of things not to like about parking garages. First of all, they can be a little spooky. Whenever I'm in one I keep expecting to see Deep Throat pop up behind a pillar. Or worse. Second, they tend to be expensive. At least around here they are. I always feel like I've got to make a choice between parking my car or sending my kids to the college of their choice. Worst of all are those garages that ask you for your keys and park your car for you. I assume I don't have to explain why that's not so hot.

I was in one of those last week. I pulled in, gave the keys to the attendant, and went to my meeting in the building next door. Three hours later I come back and give the attendant the ticket stub. He disappears into the garage and a minute later he drives my car down the ramp. Nice and slowly, carefully. Then he says—now get this—he says, "Which way will you be going, sir?" I said, "Excuse me?" He says, "Will you be turning right or left when you leave the garage?" I said, "Left." He says, "Thank you." Then he backs the car up a little bit and maneuvers it into position so it will be easier for me to make a left turn. Never seen anything like it in my life. I gave him a buck tip, which is a dollar more than I usually give.

* * *

I get a package in the mail. It's from a restaurant in New Orleans. I have no idea what it might be. I've never been to that restaurant. Never even been to New Orleans, for that matter. I open the box and it's got my class ring from college in it. I hadn't seen the ring for about fifteen years, ever since it had been stolen when my apartment was burglarized. There was a note from the manager of the restaurant apologizing for how long it had taken to track me down. If he only knew! He said that the ring had been found in one of the restrooms about two weeks before. From the outside of the ring, he knew the college and the year I graduated. From the inscription on the inside, he knew my initials. So he got in touch with the alumni office of my college, explained what he had found, and asked for a list of everyone who had graduated in 1969 and had my initials. It turns out I was the only one with those three initials, so he packed up the ring and sent it off to me. I called him to thank him and told him that if I ever got to New Orleans, I'd be sure to have dinner at his restaurant.

Imagine that—after fifteen years.

* * *

This subassembly is an important part of our product. We really have to count on the company that makes it for us. So we took a lot of time and effort with the selection process. Eventually we narrowed the list down to five possibilities, and three of us paid a visit to each of those five sites.

The first four companies we visited seemed like very competent, capable vendors. On the one hand, it made us feel good—like no matter which one we chose we probably couldn't go wrong. On the other hand, it made our choice that much tougher.

It had been a long, rough week. Five cities in five days will do that to you. We were, to put it mildly, tired. And to be perfectly honest, we really weren't looking forward to the fifth plant tour. Enough is enough, we figured.

Well, we pulled our rental car into the parking lot and followed the signs to the visitors' parking area. Then a sign on one of the visitors' parking spaces caught our eye. It said RESERVED FOR and underneath it had our company's name. We made a couple of jokes about it, but, you know, I think we all thought: "That's pretty good."

After we got inside, we were shown to an office and told that we could use it as home base for the day. Now that's not all that unusual. A lot of places set up offices for visitors, especially for visiting customers. But this one seemed warmer than usual. I don't know, less—antiseptic, I guess is the word. Like it's really used by real people. And the door of the office had a name placard for each of us.

That was all pretty nice. But what really got us was one of the things we saw on the plant tour. The factory was set up to make a run of products that were similar to our subassemblies, which was also the case in the other four plants that we had visited. I mean, that was the whole point of our making this whirlwind tour—to see potential suppliers in action turning out a similar product. But what we noticed was that the work in process was identified not just by some sort of customer code number but also by the name of the customer company—etched right on the product. None of the other four plants had done that. We asked about it and were told it was done so that everyone who works on the product knows who it's for.

We chose the fifth vendor. Now, I'm not saying that we chose those people *because* they put our names on the parking space and on the office door and on the products. But I'd be lying if I said that it didn't make a difference in our decision. Maybe none of us ever came right out and said so, but it sure as hell did.

There's No Such Thing as "Too Much Value," But There Is Such a Thing as "Trying Too Hard"

I'm real happy when people I do business with look for ways to deliver more value to me. It's a nice thing for them to do, and I'm not going to pretend that it isn't. So thanks.

Sometimes, though, people go too far, and that bugs me.

But since they're doing it for my benefit, I think I owe it to them to let them know how I feel. So here are ten attempts at adding value that I could just as well do without.

☞ 1. It would be OK with me if the people who run hotels told their maids that they didn't have to fold the last sheet of toilet paper on the roll into a little *v* when they finish cleaning up. I think they do it as a way of saying, "We've been here and checked out your toilet paper supply, and it's aces." It's a calling card. Sort of a bathroom version of the Lone Ranger's silver bullet. I suppose it's better than putting those paper strips around the toilet seat. But what bothers me is that people actually spend time thinking about those things, and I wish they'd stop because thinking about them thinking about those things gives me the creeps. Just leave me a couple of mints on my pillow at night and I'll be satisfied.

☞ 2. When businesses send out their bills, I really don't think it's necessary to have THE POST OFFICE WILL NOT DELIVER WITHOUT FIRST-CLASS POSTAGE printed in the upper-right-hand corner on the payment envelope in the little box where you're supposed to put the stamp. (And as long as I'm on the subject, do they *really* think the little box is necessary? Do you really need a target?) The way I figure it, if you're getting a bill in the mail it means you've got credit somewhere. And if you've got credit somewhere, you've probably been around enough to have a pretty good handle on the concept of "postage." It happens to be true that the post office won't deliver a letter without postage. But you'll find out soon enough, or at least as soon as the post office gets around to sending the letter back to you. So why rub it in by telling people, "You might think you can beat us out of a first-class stamp, but you've got another thing coming"?

☞ 3. I'm not sure why, but every time I hear about a money-back guarantee, the phrase "that should go without saying" comes to mind. Companies dress it all up by saying things like, "If for any reason you aren't fully satisfied with this product, we will be happy to give you a full refund." But the way I see it, that's the same thing as saying, "If it turns out that we've taken your money and held onto it for you while you tried to figure out why in the hell it was that you bought this thing that doesn't do what you thought it was going to do in the first place, then we suppose you can have your money back." Which ought to go without saying.

☞ 4. I can accept being put on hold since I understand that a tolerance for deferred gratification is a mark of maturity, and I'm willing to be more tolerant. But when you put me on hold, don't patch me into a local radio station. I know some businesses think that customers think it's better than dead air, since at least the customers will know they haven't been cut off. But depending on how many and which state lines the call is passing through, it's a practice that can give the unsuspecting caller a severe jolt of culture shock. So don't do it. And don't feed Muzak over the line either. I realize that doesn't leave a lot of options. So sue me.

☞ 5. Call me a gloomy gus, but when my son opens a present and a card falls out warning me about all the different ways that this toy could kill him, I think it puts a damper on things. I know that this is something that toy manufacturers are forced to do "for my own good" by a bunch of unpleasant consumer advocates who behave that way because they never got any toys when they were kids, but don't get me started. I just wish they'd sit down and figure out a better way.

☞ 6. Did you ever call information and have the operator come on the line and say, "This is Mary. Can I help you?" Did you *ever* wonder how the phone company managed to find so many operators named Mary? *Because they're not named Mary, that's how!* When one of them says, "This is Mary," the only thing you can be sure of is that her name isn't Mary. If her name is Mary, she'll say, "This is Jane." That's the system they have. (I'm not sure how somebody named "Mary Jane" would handle things.) I know this for a fact because my mother-in-law, who has never to the best of my knowledge really been named Mary, was named Mary for thirty-eight years while working for the phone company and she told me about it. So they should either use their real names or else hire the people who inspect clothes as operators so they can use numbers.

☞ 7. It hasn't happened yet but I won't like it the first time I find a little piece of paper in the pocket of a new shirt that says, "Inspected by Mary." Just a warning.

☞ 8. I think that it's a nice touch when garage mechanics put one of those cardboard floor mats down to help keep my car clean while they service it. I really do. But I'm willing to make a trade. You can forget about the floor mat if you promise not to leave the volume control on my radio cranked up to threshold of pain levels.

☞ 9. Why do magazines send out renewal notices six months before the subscription runs out? Or "six months after the last renewal," if you'd prefer to look at it that way. I know the notices always say that the magazine wants to make sure you don't miss out on "a single exciting issue." But it's very annoying and I wish they'd stop. If you feel the same way, here's how to fight back. The next time you get a renewal notice, tear it up and throw it away. Don't worry. You'll be getting another one soon. When it comes, throw it away too. Keep throwing renewal notices away until the magazine stops coming. (This will happen long before the renewal notices stop coming.) Then, when you get the *next* renewal notice, think of it as a handy reminder to go to the library, read the magazine for free, take the subscription card out of the magazine, and start a new sub-scription, which is always about 50 percent cheaper than renewing anyway. Serves them right for crying wolf.

☞ 10. Doctors' offices are real pacesetters when it comes to modern inventory-staging techniques. Say you have a 3:00 P.M. appointment. Sometime around 4:15 someone dressed in white (but definitely not a doctor and probably not a nurse either, so don't worry about it or it will make you crazy) will come into the waiting room, call your name, and say, "Right this way." Don't get your hopes up. The idea is to make you feel like you're making progress, which is really pretty thoughtful, but down deep you know that you're just going to wind up in some sort of holding pen for the next twenty minutes. So you might as well have stayed in the waiting room to catch up on some back issues of *The New Yorker*. Then you'll be moved to another room and told to take some of your clothes off. Someone will come in and take your temperature. Another room. More clothes off. Blood pressure. Another room. More clothes. Some sort of physicianoid will ask you, "What seems to be the trouble today?" And so on, until you eventually are given an audience with the doctor. (The experience is not unlike making your way into one of the exhibits at Disneyland.) The next time you're in a waiting room and somebody says, "Right this way," here's what to do. Say "No thanks," take off all your clothes, and announce that you'd rather just wait right there and catch up on your reading. Things will probably begin to move along at a faster pace.

Ed Bailey,
the Quality Marketing Man

Ed Bailey, the quality marketing man,
Can provide you with all the data to span
The Grand Canyonesque gap between practice and plan
When your markets don't do what the plan says they can.

Ed Bailey, the quality sales patter guy,
Can talk Bar-B-Q'd beef past a hungry hound's eye
With a wink and a nod and a line oh so sly
Till they've bought what they thought that they never would
     buy.

Ed Bailey's quality pricing analysis
Provides the security of a pants belt plus galluses
Even though it's the others whose hides must grow calluses
Since it never turns out that the "hell to be paid" hell is his.

Ed Bailey, quality ad man supreme,
Can spin out a dream of a theme that will seem
So compelling so's not to attract one small gleam
To the fact that it's all a most unseemly scheme.

Ed Bailey? He hasn't a quality clue
Of what quality marketing would bring him to do,
Past the mirrors and tricks and the smoke oh so blue
To that quality place where there's real . . . value.

7

Improving the Quality of Quality Improvement

*L*et me get this straight. Everybody buys the notion that quality is important. That improvements in quality can lead to dramatic improvements in such rather important areas as productivity, profitability, market share, and employee morale. What the hell, it may even clear up any stubbornly lingering postpubescent skin conditions in the bargain. Damn good, this quality stuff.

So tell me. Why is it so hard to implement quality improvement efforts? I mean successfully implement. I mean *really* successfully implement. And by that I don't mean squeezing out a couple of percent improvement in a couple of areas. I mean dramatic, orders-of-magnitude improvement across the board. You know, the kind of improvement that your quality consultants promised you just before you signed the contract and then realized that you had forgotten to count the silverware.

Why is it that instead of cashing in on quality improvement you find yourself involved in silly little battles like the one I had with Phil in Chapter 1 of this book? Why isn't it all so self-evidently obvious to everyone else that the only problem you should be facing is what to do with all the money and acclaim that are sure to begin rolling in?

A lot of managers have the answer. To them it's "the people," as in: "When I was coming up through the ranks, the people *cared* about the company. They *cared* about their work. They took *pride* in what they did as individuals and in what we could do together as a group. But today, hah! Today people are out to get a paycheck and that's the beginning and the end of it. That's why it's so hard to do anything about our quality problems. The people." But if those managers have really been saddled with such a grade-A bunch of goof-offs and ne'er-do-wells, then who, may we be so bold as to inquire, hired them? And who tolerates such incompetent, ineffectual performance? Such woe-is-me abdications of responsibility represent the pledge of allegiance recited each morning at the Rope Ladder School of Management, so-named because its graduates happened (apparently) to be the last few fortunates to have scrambled out of the pit of sloth and ignorance just before pulling the rope ladder up behind them.

Talk to nonmanagers and you'll get the same response—"the people"—only they're referring to a different bunch of people: "The problem is the people in management. They don't really care about quality. They just spend all day doing their little dances and playing politics and kissing each other's behinds and they forgot about what they had to do to get to where they are and what keeps 'em there: the work that the rest of us do!" But the challenge to these rank-and-file rabble-rousers might go, "If managers are so dumb and they're in charge, what does that say about you? And where's the future in sticking around a place where there are such small shoes to fill?"

I know, I know. That's a pretty petty, unexalted level at which to join the argument. But then the charges leveled against "the people," whether management or nonmanagement people, don't exactly read like a transcript from the Lincoln-Douglas debates, either. So—how to avoid such silliness? (That is what it is, after all.) The answer (no surprise here) can be found in two elements of the quality orthodoxy. The first holds that *quality is everybody's job*. What I'm talking about here is not a management/nonmanagement issue but a *leadership* issue. And anybody at any level in any functional area of an organization can be a quality leader, since leadership is taken not bestowed, and since the test of leadership is the existence of followers and not the assertion of authority.

Just where should these quality leaders focus their attention? According to the second relevant bit of quality orthodoxy, it's on the *process*, since quality is a process issue and not a people issue. More specifically, they should focus on the process by which the quality message is communicated throughout the organization.

Think of the language that is used. We talk about how hard it is to get "buy-in" to our quality efforts. We say, in our moments of more unremitting 1980s-speak, that we want everyone to "take ownership" of responsibility for quality. Well, if the leaders of an organization (managers and nonmanagers alike) want the others to *buy* and *own* quality, then they need to *sell* and *market* the quality message. Because the old adage that if you build a better mousetrap the world will beat a path to your door is, simply, untrue. You can have the best mousetrap in the world, but unless people need a mousetrap, know that they need a mousetrap, and know that you have a mousetrap to offer, you're going to have a lot of surplus inventory of mousetraps on your hands. The quality message is a powerful "product." But unless people need it, know that they need it, and know that you have it to offer, it's just going to sit on the shelf. Buy-in won't be there.

The fundamental issue is, to use the marketing term, one of "positioning." By positioning I'm talking about the simplest, clearest, crispest, most concise way to communicate the essence of the quality message throughout an organization. And the test of how the quality message is positioned is this: When people in an organization hear the word "quality," what's the first thing that pops into their minds? If it's images of excitement and success and opportunity—if the quality message is effectively positioned—then "the people" will be more than happy to buy and take ownership of quality. If not, they won't. But effectively positioning the quality message is much easier said than done. Herewith some approaches that don't work so well.

Ineffective Approach 1: Neo-Churchillian

The Neo-Churchillian approaches the issue of quality in the apocalyptic terms and world-weary tones usually reserved for declarations of war or survey articles reviewing next fall's network TV lineup. You'll know you're listening to a Neo-Churchillian in full throat when you hear:

> It has been said that "the quality of mercy is not strained." But in many organizations over the past few decades, the quality of quality has been severely strained. Almost—dare I say it?—to the breaking point.
>
> What we are talking about, my friends, is a severe "quality gap" that has become a serious problem, national in impact, global in implication.
>
> I am here to say to you today that now is not the time to show this problem any mercy! [*Here the speaker will usually do something to break new ground in xenophobic tastelessness by, say, projecting a slide showing a Japanese flag.*] I put this slide up as a reminder that, one by one, markets that have been traditionally American-dominated have fallen. That pattern, it saddens me to report, will not change. It will not change, that is, unless American attitudes change. Unless we learn to look beyond the near term . . . beyond the quarter to quarter . . . beyond the dollar for dollar . . . beyond the earnings per share. Unless we wake up and reassert the winning spirit . . . the winning attitude . . . the winning performance . . . that has always given us the winning edge. [*Here a tape recording of "Stars and Stripes Forever" is usually piped into the room, accompanied by a video montage of Wayne Newton feeding powdered milk to orphans while a baseball game is being played in the background.*]
>
> That edge will come from the people in this room—Americans all! Americans having the courage to learn from those who have gained at our expense . . . having the courage to set aside the tired

and discredited practices of the past that have put us on the wrong side of the quality gap . . . having the courage to do what it takes to reassert our rightful role at the top! Won't you join me in that journey?

Remember when Jimmy Carter returned from a long weekend at Camp David and made his "malaise" speech? Remember how the momentum from that speech swept him to victory in six out of fifty states in the 1980 election? (OK, there might have been a couple of other factors involved.) Well, the Neo-Churchillian approach to quality probably won't work quite that well for you, so you should probably think twice before using it.

Ineffective Approach 2: Crypto-Buscaglian

You can tell a Crypto-Buscaglian is on the prowl when he loosens his tie, takes off his jacket, rolls up his sleeves, and fixes everyone in the room with a look of overweening sincerity that makes *Mr. Rogers' Neighborhood* look like *Mean Streets*. Then he begins:

> I cannot begin to tell you how happy I am to have the opportunity to *share* with you this morning about the issue of quality. Because, after all, what is quality other than the essence, the inherent goodness and wonderment that lie at the heart of our noble efforts while we're on the job?!?
>
> The job of leading the way to quality is a very simple and enriching and fulfilling one, in that it involves the bringing to the surface of that essence and goodness and wonderment that resides within each of you!
>
> Some people would talk about quality in terms of competition and rivalries and the conquering of global markets [*much frowning and wincing here*]. I would like to *share* with you the notion that when people say things like that, it is something other than their essence and wonderment bubbling up to the surface!
>
> Now, I'm not passing judgment, because it's OK to be where you are! But where I want to make sure *we* are today is at the place where quality is viewed as a matter not of "how we can bring others

down by virtue of what we can do against them" but rather of "how we can lift ourselves up by virtue of what we can do together."
Let us begin!

At this point half the people in the audience begin "sharing" copies of the meeting's agenda to scope out the best time to make a break for it. The other half are worrying about what they'll do if the speaker loses it altogether and begins to ask people to hug each other and do all that other touchy-feely stuff that you thought had gone out in the 1970s. Again, an approach to be avoided.

Ineffective Approach 3: Quasi-Pavlovian

When you boil it all down, the Quasi-Pavlovian approach amounts to a single message: "If we don't do something about quality, we'll all be fired. On the other hand, if we can improve quality, we can all get rich." There's no denying the not inconsiderable advantage of simplicity, but this sort of red-meat approach can foster a rather more fevered tone than the matter would seem to call for. A useful rule of thumb: Any approach to quality that might have been embraced by Sonny Corleone is probably too intense by half to be suitable for your organization.

✳ ✳ ✳

Are these three approaches to quality exaggerated? You might think so, but I'd be willing to bet that you know somebody who has sat through speeches, presentations, meetings, or seminars that featured each of these approaches. It's not that the intentions of people taking such views of quality are wrong. Remember, quality is not a people issue, it's a process issue. And the process by which the overall tone of quality improvement efforts is established can, like any other process element, stand to be tuned from time to time. In short, the quality of quality improvement efforts should be considered and managed.

Would-be quality leaders who use these three approaches share (at least) one characteristic. They all acknowledge the need to *sell* the quality message: They recognize the need to make a strong impression on the would-be quality follower. As a result, they juice up the argument to a fairly emotional, extrarational (note: I didn't say *irrational*) level, which is necessary but dangerous. Necessary because quality improvement is a big job, and achieving it requires tapping into people's emotional as well as intellectual energies. Dangerous because such emotional, high-profile appeals for quality improvement are, by definition, conspicuous. Under the circumstances—and considering that the subject matter *is*, after all, quality—the appeal had better be right. If not, people will hear the message (the would-be leader has, after all, gone to rather great lengths to get people to sit up and take notice) and reject it. And it will be hard to recover from this setback, since first impressions count, and you can only make a first impression once.

The Neo-Churchillian approach misses the mark in that it leads to serious miscalibrations of scope. Quality is important, but it's not World War IV. *You* might want to fight them on the beaches, etc., etc., but that's not what other people signed up for. At the very least, you would seem to have some serious rewriting of job descriptions to do if you're going to take this approach.

Exponents of the Proto-Buscaglian approach run the risk of being thought of as, well, not terribly down to earth. This can introduce a rather seriously discordant note in their efforts to position quality as the ultimate real-world issue. People will be skeptical, and to make matters worse, although they might have those thoughts, they will not be inclined to *share* them. At least not with the Proto-Buscaglian.

The Quasi-Pavlovian approach is real-world, all right. *Too* real-world. Yes, it's true that to the extent that quality problems remain unresolved people may well lose their jobs. And yes, improved quality is the surest road to financial reward.

But the fact that a statement is true doesn't necessarily make it the most effective selling argument. ("Eat your vegetables, Junior, or you won't be getting the proper nutrition, and that will make you more vulnerable to several pernicious diseases that can attack your body and cause you to die a lingering and perhaps even especially painful death.") This approach makes quality scarier than it has to be, more negative than it has to be, and that's no way to *sell*.

With all three approaches the intent—to sell—is correct. But if the execution is so flawed that the would-be leader comes off sounding like (1) a goofball, (2) a flake, or (3) a doomsayer, it can be fatal to selling quality improvement efforts. Fortunately, quality leaders today manage to do a far better job of avoiding these exhortation traps. They realize that over the long haul (and quality *is* the ultimate long-haul issue) a low-profile approach wears better.

But that isn't to say there isn't a trap in the low-profile approach; it's just a different kind of trap, that's all. Which leads to . . .

Ineffective Approach 4: Technocratic (aka Proto-Nicklausian)

Here the point is best made by analogy. Let's say you are a golfer. Not a great golfer, not a terrible golfer. Just your basic can-break-a-hundred-on-a-good-day golfer. And your main problem is that you're slicing the ball. So you have a lesson with a golf pro who, after watching you hit a few screamers about 120 degrees off line to the right, tells you something like the following:

> A sliced golf ball is caused by the Bernoulli effect bringing pressure to bear on the ball in an asymmetrical fashion relative to the line of flight—to wit, when a spin is imparted around the vertical axis of a rotating sphere, the pressure on the side of the golf ball that is rotating away from the direction of flight is lowered below the level of the pressure on the side of the ball that is rotating toward the direction of flight—exponentially, not geometrically!— with the net result being a transverse pressure differential acting at

the boundary layer between laminar and turbulent flow and a net lateral pressure gradient pushing the ball off line, i.e., a slice. So stop doing that and your slicing problems will disappear.

Oh.

Understanding the physics of a golf ball in flight and knowing how to impart that knowledge to others in a way that will make them more effective at hitting nonslicing golf shots are not the same thing. In fact, if you're taking lessons from a technocrat, not only won't your slice be cured; your enthusiasm for golf may wane. You'll probably find yourself less inclined to *want* to improve. The game will be less satisfying than *ever*. Tennis will begin to be more appealing. Maybe bowling. Bocce even. Anything but this business about rotating transverse Bernoullis, or whatever in hell the pro was talking about. ("I thought I was playing a game, not studying for a Ph.D.")

Knowing the "physics" of quality is not the same thing as effectively communicating that knowledge to others. And to the extent that the knowledge is not effectively communicated, people may begin to lose whatever enthusiasm they might have had for "the game." With a purely technocratic approach to quality—one that focuses exclusively on technique and methodology and measurement and the rest—that's a risk you can run. Understand, mastering the techniques of quality is essential. But there is a difference between what you have to do and how you present it and sell it to people in the hope that they will follow your lead.

The good news is that unlike ineffective approaches 1-3, the technocratic approach involves taking an inherently lower profile. In fact, "inherently lower profile" is really a euphemism. "Boring people to death" probably comes closer to hitting the mark. It's not that it leads you to establish the *wrong* position; it's that you don't really stake out *any* position. Fortunately, since you haven't really made any impression at all, you still haven't used up your first impression. In other words, you still have a chance to make a strong first impression without having to unmake the goofball/flake/doomsayer

impression you've already made. And that is a very big advantage.

How do you go about doing so? Let's return to our golf
analogy. Effective teaching pros (as opposed to repositories
of technical minutiae) don't bog down their would-be golf en-
thusiasts in too much technical detail. In fact, they tell them
quite the opposite: "For now, forget all that business about
'left arm straight' and 'weight shift' and 'hips opening up.' Just
relax and take some nice, slow, easy swings. Let the club do
the work. Don't think golf swing. Think pendulum. Think
tempo. Think tempo. Think tempo." And all through this
soothing mantra, the golf pro will often as not be swinging,
swinging, swinging a club in slow, rhythmic arcs, establishing
a nice . . . relaxed . . . tempo.

It's not at all unusual for a golf pupil to take what is called
a "playing lesson." Pro and pupil go out on the course and
play a round of golf, with the pro dispensing pointers as various playing situations arise. Now, the pupil thinks that the
real progress gets made in such moments of explicit teaching:
"Move your right hand over a little bit on the grip. Open up
your stance just a touch. Take the club back a little to the
inside. Be sure to stay down through the shot." And to be
sure, teaching and learning do take place in these moments.
But the pro knows that the most useful part of the playing
lesson may well come as a result of the pupil seeing the pro
hit shot after shot, make swing after swing, all flowing from a
steady, consistent "tempo." The learning may be subcon-
scious, but it's there, and it's real.

None of which is to say that at some point in a golfer's
development it won't be very useful to have a fuller understanding of the technical aspects of the golf swing (or of the
flight of the golf ball itself, for that matter). What is to say is
that by focusing on tempo, providing his students with a better
feel for the game and not just a technically correct *description
of* the game, the pro will help make the pupil a better player
in the short run and will begin to instill a fuller appreciation,
understanding, and, yes, love of the game, all of which are
sure to make the pupil a better player in the long run as well.

The pro transmits not only his knowledge but his enthusiasm and passion for the game. Not a bad day's work. But first he has to establish the proper tempo.

So the question becomes: What's the tempo of quality? And once you've determined that, how do you communicate that—passion included—to people in a way that avoids the Neo-Churchillian, Crypto-Buscaglian, and Quasi-Pavlovian traps? Is there an approach to quality that establishes the proper tempo and enables the quality leader to present it in a way that is realistic (i.e., nongrandiose), down to earth (i.e., not touchy-feely), and positive and uplifting (i.e., not threatening and negative)?

Happily it can be reported that the answer is yes.

The Most Effective Approach to Positioning Quality Efforts: Ensuring the Presence of Value for Customers

The one approach to quality that meets all these demanding criteria is also the approach that flows directly from the model of quality developed in the preceding chapters of this book. I've already talked about how viewing quality from the customer's perspective will lead you, as the supplier, to see quality in terms of the presence of value as defined by the customer rather than as the absence of defects as defined by you. (Note: When I use the word "customer" I am referring to what is sometimes called the "external customer"—the person who pays money for goods and services. For some observations about the so-called "internal customer" approach, see Chapter 8.) That change in perspective can yield significant functional/operational progress in your efforts to improve quality—provided, that is, everyone in your organization gets behind those efforts. Provided, that is, that you can effectively *sell* the quality message.

That challenge becomes markedly easier when you realize that the notion at the core of the functional/operational view of quality—the presence of value—is the same one that will help you effectively sell those efforts. In other words, when you spend time dealing with the functional implications of "value to the customer," you're also reinforcing the position, selling the quality message. And when you spend time selling—establishing a value to the customer *tempo* throughout the organization—you're also reinforcing the functional/operational message. The leverage gained from such a consistent, intensely focused approach to quality can be considerable.

Does a "value to the customer" position meet the criteria listed above? I think it does.

☞ 1. It's positive, uplifting. If all the talk about quality is couched in the language of defects and limits and problems and controls, then try as you might, you will have a very hard time keeping people from translating your quality entreaties into: "Stop screwing up so much!" I know that's not what you say, and I know that's not what you intend. But it *is* what people will hear, and that's what counts. And if the stakes are (at least in a business sense) life and death, you are in effect adding the phrase "or else." Not a terribly positive platform from which to be selling. Associating quality with presence of value can help you avoid it.

☞ 2. It is down to earth. Everybody in your organization knows what it is, what it means, and what it feels like to be a customer. Whether their experience is with the local dry-cleaning store, the bank, or a vendor at work, they can relate to the notion of "value for the customer" because they've been there, they've felt it. It hits them where they live.

☞ 3. It sizes the issue appropriately. Even though the quality challenge may not be World War IV, it *is* important. When the issue is framed in such simple, straightforward terms—"What we're talking about here is making sure that our customers receive the value for which they've paid us"—it is very difficult for people to hide behind technical complexity or the smokescreen laid down by overheated rhetoric. Instead, people are forced to confront the reality that "value is what customers are after and quality is the way we can provide it." It is hard to walk away from that challenge. What's more, people *won't* walk away from such a challenge, as long as it's been properly framed for them. A "presence of value" approach to quality can provide that framing.

"Value for the customer": that's the tempo you want to establish. How do you go about doing so? There is no mystery to it, no magic formula, no blue smoke and mirrors required. The basic presumption should be that anything that will bring the customer into the forefront of people's consciousness is a good idea. Try it. Do it. Take the lead, and sell the quality message. Create a "value for the customer" position for quality in your organization.

More Ask Mr. Quality!

Dear Mr. Quality:

I'm retired now. Grew up during the Great Depression. Worked hard all my life. Too damned hard, in fact. When I was fourteen years old I held down four jobs at once. Still went to school full time. Played in the band, too. Walked eight miles to school. Swam the other three. Each way. Then my brother Daryl got accepted into medical school. The only way to pay for it was for me to get another job. But there weren't enough hours in the day. So every afternoon, I went to California and worked a job out there. Took advantage of the three-hour time difference. Sure it was tough, but I didn't complain. And I did damn fine work. High-quality work. Not like you get today. Like just the other day, I was in this restaurant. Got waited on by some young hotshot. I know he was a hotshot because he had one of those slick new seven-dollar haircuts. That's how I know. And he says to me: "You're going to order your meal and I'm going to get a tip and I don't really much care what happens to you or your meal." He says that, right to my face. He really did. Well, not in actual words and all. But I could see it in his eyes. That's what's wrong with quality nowadays. That and rock and roll.

T. Tresh

BRONX, NEW YORK

Dear Mr. Tresh:

Damn straight.

Dear Mr. Quality:

First of all, let me apologize in advance for taking issue with one of the points made in your otherwise excellent column that appeared in yesterday's paper. I feel guilty for even bringing this up, considering the fact that I have only the highest regard for you, someone who has so tirelessly and selflessly devoted his life's work to so worthwhile a cause as the promulgation of quality in the American workplace. We are all the richer for having shared our time here on this fragile orb called earth with you. But comment I must, however respectfully. To the point before us: You opined that people should be made to confront their failings and shortcomings on the job in as direct and straightforward a manner as possible. Anything more roundabout than that, you wrote, "is mollycoddling of the worst sort." Though it may be presumptuous of me to say so, my experience is that such discussions must be couched in very careful, nonthreatening terms. Otherwise any criticism, no matter how gently, constructively, or respectfully offered, will be met with suspicion and defensiveness, and that in turn will be a real obstacle to the kind of process improvement that quality progress requires. I would be honored to hear your thoughts on this matter.

H. Clarke

BRONX, NEW YORK

Dear "Mr." Clarke:

If you think you know so much about quality, let me ask *you* a question: Just how many newspapers does *your* column appear in every day? Come on, Clarke, tell me—how many?!?

Dear Mr. Quality:

I can't begin to tell you how exciting it's been to hop aboard the quality bandwagon. In fact, we've just introduced a new quality program that we're particularly proud of. We call it The Quality Hour. Every day, Monday through Friday, from 1:00 P.M. to 2:00 P.M., we all redouble our efforts to improve quality. As the company's CEO, I realize that it's especially important for me to do everything I can to make this program a big success. So I spend the hour visiting as many departments as I can, exhorting people by saying things like, "Come on, come on everyone. Let's all do our level best!" And, "Hip hip hooray! Today let's improve quality!" And (my particular favorite), "When the going gets tough, why not just buckle down and give it even a bit more effort all around?" I guess you can tell why I get so "up" for The Quality Hour. It's so exhilarating! My question for you is: Should I be doing more to get involved in our quality efforts?

R. Houk

BRONX, NEW YORK

Dear Mr. Houk:

No. In view of what you've told me, I think you're doing quite enough already.

Dear Mr. Quality:

Like, I've just been working for about three, four months, OK? And just the other day I came up with a pretty neat idea and I thought I'd tell you what it was, so here's the neat idea I had. Instead of making us stand in line for five minutes at the end of the day to punch out, throw away the time cards and let us go home five minutes early. It is my hope to leverage ideas like this into a management trainee position.

F. Peterson

BRONX, NEW YORK

P.S. Tool-and-die making is my life.

Dear Mr. Peterson:

Do you realize that you're just a short drive on the Deegan Expressway from being able to study at the knee of Mr. Tresh?

Dear Mr. Quality:

What do you get when you cross a quality control inspector with a vice-president of manufacturing on the last day of a quarter?

R. Repoz

BRONX, NEW YORK

Dear Mr. Repoz:

A job opening in the quality control department.

Dear Mr. Quality:

I've been working under the impression that it's management's job to lead the way to quality by creating an environment—a corporate culture, if you will—that is conducive to a sharing, nurturing, empowering climate of intrapreneurial excellence. Am I right, or what?

R. Terry

BRONX, NEW YORK

Dear Mr. Terry:

Almost. It's management's job to create such a sharing, nurturing, empowering climate of intrapreneurial excellence in tidy little one-minute chunks.

Dear Mr. Quality:

A friend told me, "You've gotta sell quality. If it sounds too 'official' people won't buy it." He says, "If they made BINGO a sacrament, attendance would drop off." I'm not quite sure what he meant by that, but he was so darned sincere when he said it that I just had to listen. So what we did was we instituted a weekly Quality Beer Blast every Friday. You know, borrowed a page from those companies out there in what you call your "Silicone Valley." It seems to be working out OK. Sure we make a helluva lot more mistakes on Friday afternoons, but who cares?

J. Kenney

BRONX, NEW YORK

Dear Mr. Kenney:

Perhaps you should make the beer blasts officially required. Then attendance will fall off and your Friday quality will improve.

Dear Mr. Quality:

When they make a mistake, hurt 'em. Bad.

G. G. Liddy

BEHIND THE POTTED PALM
ANYTOWN, USA

P.S. No reply necessary.

Dear Mr. Quality:

I can understand our management people wanting to improve quality and all. But I thought that their recent Increase Quality or We'll Shoot Your Dog campaign was a bit heavy-handed. Wouldn't you agree?

H. Lopez

BRONX, NEW YORK

Dear Mr. Lopez:

By any chance, you didn't just move to the Bronx from Anytown, USA, did you?

This Too Shall Pass

A Tragicomedy in One Act

[*The setting is an out-of-the-way corner of a company cafeteria. It is late morning—just before lunchtime, but too late for coffee klatching. Thus, no people. The furniture, such as it is, is of the late-1950s Festive School, with semiseedy formica table tops, plastic chairs dyed a variety of colors most of which do not exist in nature, and table legs shimmed up with those silvery-cardboard ashtrays folded over just the precise amount to render the tables almost but not quite level. The ambience is not unlike that encountered in a moderately successful laundromat.*]

[*On each table is a laminated tent card—similar to the cards that advertise overpriced "Contrails Cocktails" in airport lounges and overgreased fried clam specials on interstate rest-stop-cum-diners. The only discernible legend on these tent cards, though, is a large, stylized, rather cryptic* **Q**.]

[*A man carrying a tray enters from stage right. His name is Earl. Earl has, how shall we say, been around the track a few times. In a less enlightened era we might have referred to him as a late-middle-aged or senior employee—characterizations that Earl would have objected to only because of their inherent wimpiness. ("Codger aspiring to geezer" is how Earl would describe himself, proudly.)*]

[*Earl places his tray on a table, pulls out a chair, and sits down. He begins to eat his lunch, staring straight ahead silently. After about thirty seconds, he turns his gaze slightly left. He picks up the Q tent card and bobs it in his hand as*] *though he were trying to guess its weight (which, in a sense, he is). After due consideration, he lets out a barely audible snort, returning the card to its original position next to the three mismatched salt shakers, and continues to eat his lunch.*]

[*From stage right another man enters, also carrying a lunch tray. His name is Ed. Ed places his tray on the table and takes the seat directly across from Earl, who doesn't so much as acknowledge Ed's arrival. Earl and Ed are contemporaries, and it's very clear that this is not the first time they've shared a cafeteria table. In fact, their actions have the word "ritual" written all over them.*]

[*Hungrily, Ed digs into his bowl of split pea soup. Earl looks at him with the kind of admiration reserved for people who "dig into" split pea soup of any kind, much less that served in a company cafeteria. Then he speaks.*]

EARL: How's the soup?

ED: My soup?

EARL: [*Looking around broadly*] Yeah, your soup! You see anybody else in here?

ED: Soup's fine. Why do you ask?

EARL: I dunno. Just wondering. Hot enough?

ED: [*On his guard*] Yeah, it's hot enough, I guess.

EARL: Salted just right? You don't want too much salt, or too little. Just the right amount?

ED: [*Even more warily*] Yeah, just the right amount of salt.

EARL: The texture—how about the texture? Texture's an important part of the pea soup experience. You figure the texture is about as it should be?

ED: Yes, goddammit, the texture is fine! What the hell are all these soup questions about, anyway?

EARL: I'm just trying to get into the spirit of things. [*He nods toward the Q tent card.*] I just want to make sure that the overall *quality* of the soup is up to our demanding standards, that's all. After all [*as though reading from a pre-*

pared speech] quality is a matter of the utmost concern for everyone in any position throughout the company.

[Ed stares at Earl. He's puzzled, but the light is beginning to dawn. He looks at the Q tent card, then back at Earl. Four seconds pass. Then the light clicks on. Brightly. Ed bursts out laughing and in the process releases a spray of split pea soup onto the tray in front of him.]

EARL: *[Lurching back in his chair]* Gee-zus! What is this—a scene from *The Exorcist?!?*

ED: *[Beginning to get it back under control]* I'm sorry, I'm sorry! *[He wipes his mouth with the napkin from his tray, then takes several more napkins from the dispenser at the end of the table to mop up the tray itself. With one last napkin, he dabs at his eyes, which are moist from laughter.]* It was just funny, that's all.

EARL: As funny as what went on in here yesterday afternoon?

ED: You may have a point.
[Earl picks up the Q tent card and holds it in front of him.]

EARL: You think that by now they'd learn to save their money on this kind of nonsense.

ED: *[He has now fully composed himself.]* I don't know. I kind of agree with what they were saying about quality. I think it *is* as important as they said it is.

EARL: You think *I* don't agree with that?!? Hell, of course quality is important. But that's my whole point. It's too damned important to treat it like another one of their goddamned pep rallies. "The future of the company is at stake, so let's order some balloons and bumper stickers and everything will be all right." Unbelievable.

ED: Aren't you being a little unfair? Don't you think they want the new Q-program to work?

EARL: Of course I think they want it to work. That's what makes me so nervous. They might actually *do* some of the things they talked about. And when you've been around as long as I have—as long as *we* have—you just know what sort of stuff will work and what sort of stuff won't, that's all I'm saying. And this [*shaking the Q tent card, then putting it down*] won't work.

ED: I don't suppose you also think you're being just a little self-righteous.

EARL: I don't know about righteous, but I know that I'm right. What's more, *you* know that I'm right. You can't say it because of your position in the company. I understand that and respect it, I guess. But your little soup-spritzing act told me all I need to know about what you really think.

[*This time it's Ed who picks up the Q tent card and studies it. Earl has resumed eating his lunch. Twenty, maybe thirty seconds pass.*]

ED: Maybe it'll be different this time. [*He puts the Q tent card back on the table.*]

EARL: Maybe it will. But give me one good reason why that might be the case.

ED: Because it's too important not to work this time.

EARL: Oh, you mean like when they made a big thing out of proclaiming the Corporate Mission? "It is our avowed Corporate Mission to, within the next five years, become the undisputed leader in our industry based on three fundamental performance indicators: growth, market share, return on shareholders' equity." Nice mission statement. I still remember it. Remember the slogan, too: "All for 1!" Of course, it's easier to remember that sort of thing when you're not distracted by anyone asking you to actually *do* anything about it. But it was a damn nice mission statement and a damn fine slogan. Kinda gives you a little gooseflesh when you hear them, doesn't it?

ED: [*Fighting to keep a smile from breaking through*] People are entitled to a misstep now and then. They may be in top management, but they're only human.

EARL: I understand that. And everybody else understands that, too. Hell, people will put up with a lot of mistakes. But the problem is that this business about being "only human" cuts both ways. You can't keep asking people to saddle up their horses and take the hill, and then say to them, "Oh, never mind." You just can't keep doing that to people. Sooner or later, they're going to tune you out. After all, "they're only human."

[*It's clear that Ed feels obliged to defend management. It's also clear that his heart isn't in it, since he agrees with what Earl is saying.*]

ED: But that's still just one other example.

EARL: OK. You want more examples? I'll give you more examples. Who was in yesterday's meeting up here?

ED: I don't know. Pretty much everybody I guess.

EARL: Everybody?

ED: Well, everybody from supervisory levels on up.

EARL: Yeah, right. I seem to remember that one of the main points that they made was that quality has got to be viewed as *everybody's* job. That quality was "the ultimate team sport." Wasn't that it?

ED: Yeah, something like that.

EARL: Well, what the hell kind of team sport is it when half the players aren't asked to come to the game?

ED: But they were all told to take the message back to their people.

EARL: Oh, the people got the message all right. They got it when the memo went out to "All Managers and Supervisors."

ED: I happen to know that the reason that everyone wasn't invited was purely a practical consideration. All our employees can't fit in the cafeteria at the same time, that's all. It wasn't any more sinister than that.

EARL: I didn't say it was sinister. Just stupid, that's all.

Choose your poison. I don't know—I'm not privy to all the behind-the-scenes discussions. [*Ed gives him a look of friendly annoyance.*] Maybe it does make sense. In fact, if their objective is to get things to the point where the entire employee population can fit in this cafeteria, then I'd say they're going about it just right. It reminds me of the old joke about the Army: "There will be no mail or liberty until morale improves around here!"

[*Ed feels that he can safely laugh at this and does. Once again he picks up the Q tent card.*]

Ed: There have been some real beauties of programs around here, haven't there?

Earl: Oh, geez. Tell me about it.

Ed: How about when we went through those three straight quarters where we actually lost money? When was that—about six or seven years ago?

Earl: That sounds about right.

Ed: Yeah. So they come up with some program having something to do with "profits." What did they call it? The Three P's or something like that, wasn't it?

Earl: P-Cubed.

Ed: Yeah, P-Cubed! That was it: Profit Performance Program.

Earl: God, that was a classic. Remember all the lectures about "what profit is" and "the difference between price and cost"?

Ed: [*Nodding*] Remember what Jerry Donovan stood up and said at one of those meetings?

Earl: I remember that it was good, but I don't remember what it was.

Ed: He got up—in front of all the top dogs—he got up and said: "I think we got the idea that there's supposed to be a difference between the number that represents price and the number that represents cost. Now why don't you all go back and see if you can't come to some agreement about which one is supposed to be bigger."

[*At this they both break up laughing.*]

EARL: That's right! Now I remember. [*He stops laughing, but continues smiling.*] That Jerry was a funny guy.

ED: Whatever happened to him, anyway?

EARL: I don't know. Wasn't long after that that he, uh, "left" here though, was it?

ED: No, it wasn't.

EARL: Gee, imagine that.

ED: [*Ignoring Earl's last comment*] My all-time favorite program was the one that the sales manager came up with to get his sales force to treat all the backup people in the office a little better.

EARL: I don't think I ever heard of that one.

ED: You didn't? Oh, it was another classic. The sales reps had a reputation for being prima donnas. Well deserved, I might add. Anyway, the sales manager was getting a lot of complaints from the secretarial and administrative staff about how their efforts weren't appreciated. So he decides to run a program to make sure that his reps don't take the support staff for granted.

EARL: I don't know. That doesn't sound like such a bad idea to me.

ED: It's not a bad idea at all. But do you know what he names the program?

EARL: I'm afraid to guess.

ED: He calls it—get ready—the Take a Grunt to Lunch program.

EARL: Are you kidding me?!?

ED: [*Laughing*] No, I'm not! Take a Grunt to Lunch. Honest to God. Do you think I could think of something like that on my own?

EARL: [*Shaking his head*] I think maybe the problem is sloganitis. People get so caught up in being cute or clever that they forget about just what it is that they're trying to accomplish. I've got a slogan for the Q-Program. Wanna hear it?

ED: I'll probably regret this, but shoot.

EARL: How does this sound to you? "The closer we get to the end of the quarter, the farther away you should stay." Pretty good, no?

ED: Honest, maybe. But not much of a slogan.

EARL: I don't know, I think it's pretty good. Better than the new slogan for the company's Wellness/Civic Responsibility Program that the HR types cooked up: "Aerobics for Peace" or some goddamn thing.

ED: Remind me to stay away from that one.

EARL: You and me both. [*He finishes the last bite of his lunch. Ed has been done for a while, since all he had was the pea soup — what was left of it.*] Forget about the slogans. I think what's really got me scared about the Q-Program is the way I see them going about it.

ED: Specifically?

EARL: Well, from what I understand, some sort of corporate quality consultant is going to go around to each department, right?

ED: Right. That's part of it.

EARL: Yeah. So right off the bat I have a problem with somebody saying to me: "I'm from corporate and I'm here to help you." Know what I mean?

ED: I suppose I do, yes. [*This time he's unsuccessful in his efforts to suppress a smile.*]

EARL: So we've got this weenie from corporate coming around to tell me how to do my job better, but the first thing he does is ask me what my job is. Now I'm no "quality consultant," but it seems to me if they're gonna be any help, it would be a good idea if they knew what the job was before they started poking around giving advice. Do you agree?

ED: No comment.

EARL: Maybe I ought to volunteer to help them do *their* jobs better! That can be my contribution to the Quality Program. I mean, what the hell. I seem to have the necessary qualifications. I have no bloody idea what it is that *they* do. Whattya think?

ED: I don't.

EARL: You don't? What do you mean?

ED: I mean that you're getting yourself all worked up over nothing. I mean that considering how long you've been around here, you ought to know better. I mean that it isn't worth it. And do you know why?

EARL: Why?

ED: Because . . . [*He looks around the room and then looks back at Earl. For the first time, his tone and expression are completely unguarded*] . . . this too shall pass.

EARL: This too shall pass?

ED: [*Nodding*] This too shall pass. Trust me.

[*Ed picks up his tray and exits stage right. Earl watches him depart. He then picks up the Q tent card and studies it. Shaking his head, he puts the card back down next to the three salt shakers. Curtain.*]

The Secret to
Selling Quality to Employees

You know the need.
They need to know.
You want to sell.
They want to buy.
They ask you how.
You give them answers.
But *how*'s not the question.
The question is *why*?

A Dash of Heresy . . .
Just to Spice Things Up

I think it's safe to say that all the ideas presented so far in this book have been consistent with the consensus truths surrounding the topic of quality—notions like "Quality is everybody's job," and "Quality is a process issue, not a people issue," and "Quality should be designed in, not tacked on as an afterthought." Up to this point, any deviation from the quality orthodoxy is a matter of miscommunication on my part rather than one of intent. (In other words, it's a process issue, not a people issue.)

But there is one broadly accepted notion connected to quality with which I would now like to, respectfully, take issue. And although it's not so much a fundamental philosophical matter as it is a tactical one, it's a tactic that is so commonly accepted that criticism of it may be perceived as crossing the line to dabble in heresies.

The notion? That of the *internal customer*.

The heresy? The internal customer model doesn't work as well as a lot of people think. Or more precisely, even though it may help solve a minor problem, it can compound a much more major one.

I will pause here to wait for the heavens to rumble, the earth to shake, and other suitably biblical reactions. All I ask is that you read the rest of this chapter before calling for the inquisition to begin.

✳ ✳ ✳

The internal customer model is commonly recommended, widely used. Basically, it says the following:

The workings of any organization can be thought of as a series of transactions between "internal suppliers" and "internal customers." John does his job and in the process produces some sort of work product, which in turn is used by Mary to do her job and produce her work product, which in turn is used by Jim to do his job and produce his work product. Etc., etc., etc. According to the internal customer model, Mary is John's internal customer, and Jim is Mary's internal customer. (John and Mary are the internal suppliers to, respectively, Mary and Jim.)

Maybe the business is a sandwich shop. John's job is to slice the cold cuts. Mary's job is to assemble the sandwiches and fill the orders brought to her by Jim, the waiter. Maybe it's an accounting department, and it's John's job to collect the monthly travel-and-expense reports from the regional offices and deliver them to Mary, who boils that raw data into a summary report for Jim, who uses it in preparing a monthly operating statement for the division as a whole. Maybe it's a personnel department, and it's John's job to screen initial applicants for a job, Mary's job to interview the people appearing on the list of ten names provided by John, and Jim's job to make a selection from the list of three finalists provided by Mary. Whatever. The whole idea is that as the member of an organization you should think of yourself as the supplier to the next person in the process, who is your internal customer. Then, extending that premise, you simply do all the things you need to do to ensure that you deliver a quality product to your "customer."

That model would seem to be logical enough. It takes a

process view of things. It maintains an emphasis on "value to the customer," and this book has certainly talked value to the customer until the cows come home. So what's the problem? Seems like that ought to work, doesn't it?

It might seem so. But consider the planted axioms inherent in the internal customer model.

Planted axiom 1: "Everybody in an organization doesn't re-ally come into contact with the customer."

Obviously there are some jobs for which the connection to the customer (read: *external* customer) is much more direct and conspicuous than for others. If you're in sales, or wait on tables, or punch a cash register in a supermarket checkout line, it's easier to see the connection to your organization's customers than if you work in, say, the MIS department, closeted away in some godforsaken headquarters building, protected from such untidy concepts as "customers" and "markets." But the fact that the connection isn't as obvious doesn't mean that it's any less real. And the fact that you may not be able to *see* the effects of your actions on customers doesn't mean that those effects don't exist.

Suppose your daughter has to undergo some diagnostic tests in your local hospital. As part of the admissions process, you must answer a number of questions put to you by a clerk in the admissions department, who reads them off a computer screen and types in your responses right on-line at a computer keyboard. As the customer in this situation (and you *are* paying the bill, so you *are* the customer), what do you suppose your frame of mind would be like? How tolerant of bureaucratic nonsense do you suppose you would be?

Now, the forms used by the admissions clerk were designed by one of the software specialists on the hospital staff (i.e., someone from the MIS department). Knowing that, would you prefer that the software specialist had developed the forms operating from the mind set that the admissions clerk was the customer or that *you* were the customer? In other words, would you prefer that the form delivered the optimum value to you or to the clerk? Do you suppose that the difference in that mind set might result in a difference in the design of that form? Damn right it would. Do you suppose you might notice that difference? Damn right you would. Do software specialists come into contact with the customer? Damn right they do. *

Planted axiom 2: "The dynamics of the transaction between a supplier and an internal customer are the same as the dynamics between a supplier and an external customer."

I suppose this *might* be true in a business where real money doesn't change hands and customers don't have any real choice as to which supplier they can use. (Although even here this may not work.) But in most instances, it simply isn't the case.

You may be the director of marketing, and you may have to do business with your company's in-house advertising department. In other words, it could be argued that you are the ad department's internal customer. But you don't pay the department in real money. (Sorry, but accounting conventions like "allocations" and "charge-backs" to cover the costs of maintaining such an in-house department are fundamentally different from paying real money to an outside advertising agency.) Even more important, what do you do when you're dissatisfied with the results you get from that in-house advertising department? Do you throw them out? Take your busi-

---

*In the spring of 1988 I participated in a series of seven seminars involving all the managers and supervisors of a large service corporation in the Midwest. At the beginning of each session, those attending the seminar filled out a questionnaire. One of the questions asked was: "Does what you do on the job have an impact on the company's customers?" In all seven cases, at least 60 percent answered "No." In one case the number was *80 percent!* Now, if the managers in an organization don't think in terms of their effect on the customer, what do you suppose the chances are that the rank and file workers in that organization will? It is precisely that kind of obliviousness to what goes on outside the walls of the organization that is in itself a serious process problem, and it is a problem that will not be helped—and can be exacerbated—by the internal customer model.

ness elsewhere? Maybe accept a competitive bid from the folks down in shipping and receiving? Of course you don't. You have all kinds of spirited little battles over who has authority over what, when, where, and how much. Dynamic, yes. The *same* dynamic, no.

Understand: This is not to argue that it's either a good or a bad idea to maintain an in-house advertising department. It's merely to say that the dynamics are *different* from what they are in a *real* customer/supplier relationship and that it's silly to pretend otherwise. For one thing, in a true supplier/customer relationship, the supplier is subordinate to the customer, which is as it should be. Please note that subordinate doesn't mean "fawning" or "obsequious" or, if you prefer a somewhat more vulgar adjective, "round-heeled." It's merely a way of acknowledging just who, after all, is paying money to whom, a way of indicating that the supplier is the supplier only at the sufferance of the customer.

The question for those who would use the internal customer model: Do you really want to set up a dynamic in your organization where one group is made to feel subordinate to another (irrespective, that is, of standard, hierarchical reporting relationships)? The usual reply: "But we go out of our way to discourage the notion that the supplier is subordinate to the (internal) customer." Oh *really?!?* And just how, may I ask, do you manage to remind your people that when it's a *real* customer, they really are subordinate? "Oh, well, uh, they just remember, because, uh, that's the real customer and all and not the internal customer, and there's a difference and they, uh, just do, that's how." Oh.

But back to our example. So you're the marketing director and that makes you the internal customer of your internal advertising people, because, after all, they provide you with the ads and other material to promote your products. But in order for the in-house advertising people to create those ads and brochures, they have to count on the people in your department for the necessary product expertise and market knowledge. In other words, *they* are *your* customers as well. And both you and the ad people count on various reports and other financial information from the good folks in accounting, which makes both of you the customers of accounting. Of course, since accounting people need accurate budget and forecasting information from both you and advertising, they are your customers, too. And on and on it goes, until at some point reality clears its throat, taps you on the shoulder, and the notion of the internal customer ceases to be a useful model in that it adds to the complexity rather than subtracts from it.

Planted axiom 3: "The internal customer model will cause people to elevate their co-workers to the exalted status they normally reserve for customers."

That is an appealing notion. So appealing, in fact, that it seems a quibble to point out how wrongheaded it is. Call it Gresham's Law as applied to word usage: "Bad usage drives out good." It's tempting to think that by calling your co-workers "customers" you will begin to assume that they are sanctified by grace and automatically treat them with a corresponding degree of reverence. But that's not the way it works. What really happens is that, because the word "customer" gets used every time anybody so much as hands anybody else a paper clip, it will eventually cease to be a special word, cease to connote a special concept—which is about 180 degrees out of phase with what ought to happen. Customers—*real* customers—*are* special. When people hear the word "customer," bells ought to go off in their heads to make them respond appropriately. But they're not going to respond appropriately if they keep hearing false alarms—if they keep hearing talk about how Frieda in accounting and Ernie on the loading dock are their customers.

Planted axiom 4: "If Point A connects to Point B, Point B connects to Point C, Point C connects to Point D, and so on, then you will necessarily have a line pointing exactly to where you want it to point."

You may want to assume that if each function delivers value to its internal customer, the maximum amount of value will necessarily be delivered to the external customer, but you'll have probably made better assumptions in your life. Here's the test. You're standing on the ledge of a burning building. Fifteenth floor. Below you are two separate groups of firefighters, each one holding a net for you to jump into. The net on the left was made by a company that faithfully used the internal customer model, with every department taking great pains to deliver that which was considered to be of value by the next department in the process. The net on the right was made by a company that took great pains to make sure that everyone understood one basic fact: "We're here to build nets that will catch people jumping from the fifteenth floor of burning buildings."

Which net would you jump into? Me too.

The "Point A to Point B to Point C" business is part of the core curriculum at the Conga Line School of Management: Everyone is connected to everyone else, and you're moving, so it feels like progress, but nobody's really going anywhere in particular.

Planted axiom 5: "Ultimately, the process that must be managed is the process by which all the various departments in an organization function together."

Quality is a process issue, and one process that must be managed is the way work is carried on throughout the organization. To be sure, that is a very broad perspective to take. It's a process that itself comprises literally thousands upon thousands of subprocesses down through various levels of resolution: group, division, department, function, task, subtask, and so on. But it's possible to take a step back and view things from an even broader perspective. *Fundamentally, the process that must be managed is the process by which the organization as a whole provides value to its customers.* From that point of view, all the activities within the organization become subprocesses. The use of the internal customer model is in itself a part of the process. *And to the extent that the internal customer model causes people to define the fundamental process at hand too narrowly, it in itself becomes the source of a serious process problem.*

✳ ✳ ✳

In the push and pull of organizational life, it can be easy to forget a very basic fact: namely, that your business organization exists for the purpose of delivering value to your customers. When you face a hundred separate internal-to-the-organization issues every day and have time to do only twelve of them, and your organization's customers aren't beating on you but your boss is, it's not hard to guess where the attention will go, not hard to see how an internal focus might evolve. It's not a people issue; it's a process issue. And under the circumstances, a vitally important part of the process ought to be the drawing of bright, bold lines around the notion of "customer," and the avoidance of *anything* that tends to blur or dull those lines.

And that's where the internal customer concept goes wrong. I'm not saying that you shouldn't care about your co-workers, that you shouldn't try to deliver value to your co-workers, that you shouldn't do everything you can to make sure that the process by which you work together functions as smoothly and effectively as possible. I am saying, simply, that there's a difference between customers and co-workers and that difference should be made very clear to all concerned.

"But isn't this only a matter of semantics?" I hear that argument a lot, and the part that I frankly find dumbfounding is the implication that "if all we're talking about are words, then it can't be all that important." Well, it *is* a matter of semantics. All we're talking about *are* words. But words matter. A lot. The issue is one of enabling an organization to operate with a very clear focus, a very clear sense of purpose. As a metaphor, "internal customer" is not without usefulness. But as a model to drive day-to-day business action, it is, if I may be so bold as to suggest, almost breathtakingly arrogant. Its implicit premise is this: "Our business organization is the permanent fixture, the constant; thus we can bend the notion of 'customer' to fit our purposes."

Consider the opposite approach, one that holds: "It's the customer who is the constant; our organization is inherently temporary. That being the case, we will bend the organization to suit the purposes of the customer."

Now ask yourself: Which organization is more likely to be permanent and which one temporary?

Johnson's Formal Wear

A Case Study in Applying the Internal Customer Model

Johnson's Formal Wear is in the business of renting formal clothing—tuxedos, dinner jackets, and all associated accessories—to men. The lion's share of its business comes from weddings and proms. (June is a very busy month at Johnson's Formal Wear.) With fifty-three retail stores (locations owned and operated by Johnson's) and twenty-two other locations (usually department stores in smaller cities that rent formal wear to customers through the services of Johnson's), Johnson's is the largest formal wear rental company in the state.

Orders placed at any of these seventy-five locations are filled at the company's central Service Center. Comprising a warehouse, laundry and dry-cleaning facilities, and various administrative departments, the Service Center accounts for the majority of the costs and overhead incurred in the Johnson's operation. Included in these costs are the shipping charges associated with sending a piece of clothing to any of the Johnson's outlets. Under the accounting systems in place at Johnson's, such charges count against the performance of the Service Center.

Recently, this has been a source of contention within the organization. The issue becomes especially controversial when significant incremental costs are involved. Suppose, for example, that a couple decides on Thursday morning to get married on Saturday. (Yes, that really does happen.) The groom then shows up at Johnson's on Thursday afternoon and wants his formal clothing by noon on Friday. Assuming that the proper size and style are in stock and available to fill the order, the Service Center may well have to pay someone to work overtime to do the laundering, dry cleaning, and pressing, someone else to do the tailoring, and someone else to do the necessary order processing, packing, and shipping. With a Friday noon delivery deadline, the clothing cannot go out on a normally scheduled truck route. It must be sent via an overnight delivery service. Incremental cost to the Service Center: $18.00 of overtime pay plus a $35.00 overnight delivery charge. On a rental that cost the impetuous groom just $60.00.

Needless to say, such rush deliveries tend to put a squeeze on Johnson's profit margins. They also put a squeeze on Ellen Wojzahowicz, manager of the Service Center. As Ellen puts it:

> It really just boils down to an issue of fairness. I get paid for financial performance. Sure, there's a lot of talk about the importance of service and quality and all that, but when the time comes to give out raises or promotions or decide whose job is secure and who is expendable, what management looks at is the financial contribution of the Service Center. And any way you slice it, when one of these rush orders comes in here, we get whacked. Overtime charges, shipping charges—not to mention the way all our other work goes to hell in a handbasket while we scramble to fill the order. Why should we be penalized for something over which we have no control? And the better we do our job, the more we get penalized. We could use a cheaper delivery service and take a chance, but that just goes against the grain. It just isn't right, isn't fair, that's all.

Ellen's points are well taken by Art Paine, District Sales Manager for eleven of Johnson's stores. But he has concerns of his own:

I realize that Ellen has to eat a lot of extra costs when we take on a rush order like that. And I know that we don't make any money on those orders—probably lose money, in fact. But a guy comes in here and says, "I'm getting married the day after tomorrow. I want to look nice. I gotta have a suit by Friday!" What am I supposed to do, tell him I'm sorry, but we don't want his business? Maybe taking on that kind of order costs us a few bucks in the short run, but we'd lose a lot more if we turned away that business. Word of mouth and reputation are very important in this business. We don't want people going around saying bad things about us. So we fill the orders.

Clearly, both sides can make a perfectly reasonable, perfectly rational case. But just as clearly, it is causing bad blood between the stores and the Service Center. Something must be done, and the responsibility seems to lie with Ron Robinson, Johnson's Vice-President of Field Operations and the person to whom both Wozjahowicz and Paine report. In Ron's words:

It's an untenable situation. Ellen is frustrated at the way the accounting system is set up, but what she sees is Art and his people sending her orders that are taking money out of her pocket. Art figures that he's just doing his job, and he really doesn't want to have to spend his time listening to Ellen complain about the fact that he's getting orders. There's a resentment there, and the resentment then carries over into other areas. Soon the whole relationship between the stores and the Service Center sours. And that's not good for anybody: for Ellen, for Art, or for Johnson's. I guess I've got to get involved.

Let's look at three different approaches to resolving the cost-allocation problem at Johnson's Formal Wear.

SCENARIO A

[*Ron meets with Ellen and tells her that he has decided to employ the internal customer model. He wants Ellen and her employees to think of all Johnson's rental outlets as the cus-*

tomers of the Service Center. That being the case, the extra rush order charges must just be thought of as part of the cost of doing business. However, Ron does agree to consider making whatever accounting adjustments might be necessary to ensure that Ellen's performance ratings are not unfairly affected by things like rush order charges. Six months later, they review the results.]

ART: As far as I can tell, Ron did about the only logical thing that he could have done. I've always thought of myself as the customer of the Service Center—I place an order and the center sends me product. That sounds like what it means to be a customer to me. But I've never felt like I, the customer of the Service Center, have been treated as well as I treat the people who come into my stores. I don't know. Maybe because I'm in sales I'm more naturally sensitive to the customer. Maybe the people who work in the Service Center need that kind of reminder. I think this "internal customer" business might just do the trick.

ELLEN: OK. So now Art is my customer. I accept that. So maybe I ought to think about raising my prices, to offset some of those costs of doing business that Ron talked about. But I can't *really* do that. At least that's what I'm told. Then maybe I can refuse to accept an order. That's what I think the stores ought to do when somebody comes in and expects overnight service. But I'm not allowed to do *that*, either. So I guess what this means is that when Art says, "Jump," I'm supposed to ask, "How high?" I'm supposed to tell all my people that "the stores are our customers" and that it's our job "to give those customers the kind of service they deserve." Well, hell. We've been giving good service to the stores. That's not the issue. I guess I'm not sure just what all this internal customer business is supposed to accomplish.

RON: Things haven't really been working out as well as we had hoped. There's still a lot of bad blood. To be honest, if anything the situation might be a little worse. And when all is said and done, we've still got people coming in and wanting next-day delivery, and we're losing our shirts in the process—no pun intended. Sure, we can make some adjustments to our systems so that Ellen and the Service Center aren't unfairly marked down. That's being done. But I still don't feel like we've gotten to the heart of the matter. It still doesn't feel quite right to me.

SCENARIO B

[Ron meets with Art and the other district managers and tells them he wants them to think of the orders they deliver to the Service Center as their product and Ellen, in her capacity as Service Center manager, as their customer. That being the case, it is their responsibility to ensure the quality of their product. Orders delivered to the Service Center must meet certain criteria for completeness, accuracy, clarity, and lead time. If they don't, Ellen can refuse to accept the orders. That is, she can reject a store's "product," citing quality deficiencies as the cause. Six months later, they review the results.]

ELLEN: Now we're getting somewhere. This is the first time since I've been here that we've really gotten to the root cause of a problem. We do good work here at the Service Center—quality work. Always have. What screws up the process are all the curves that get thrown at us from the stores. But this approach makes sense. It's like we're running a factory here. If you get bad raw materials in a factory, you can refuse to accept shipment. That way, quality doesn't suffer. The orders that come in from the stores are our raw materials. The quality we produce can't ever get any better than the quality of the raw materials—the quality of the orders. Now we can refuse to accept shipment, and that will really help us keep the quality levels where they ought to be.

ART: This is nuts. I've got people coming in here who want to give us their money, and I have to tell them that I can't take it because some people back in some *warehouse* who don't know the first thing about what it's like out here in the real world have decided that they just don't have enough time to do things "just right." Well, here's what doing things "just right" is doing for us. The penmanship on the order forms is now "just right." And the measurements that we take are now "just right." And the lead time that we give the warehouse to fill the order is "just right." The only thing that isn't "just right" is that fewer and fewer people are renting our clothes. Of course, that ought to increase the satisfaction of our internal customer, since life in a warehouse is probably a lot more comfortable when there's nothing coming in or going out. I shoulda gone into the aluminum siding business like my brother-in-law wanted me to, that's what I shoulda done.

RON: I always thought that paying attention to quality was supposed to make things better—that we were supposed to make more money. The one good thing is that our costs have gone down. But that's just because sales have dropped off. Hell, I can get our costs down to zero in a hurry if that's all we want to do. All we have to do is close up shop and get out of the business—which is the direction we seem to be heading in. Even that would be an improvement, since it would mean I wouldn't have to deal with any more of the crap that's been going on between the stores and the Service Center.

SCENARIO C

[*Ron decides to take a drastic step: He talks to some customers. Not the woman in the hallway who asks him for the correct time. Or the man who asks him for the salt in the cafeteria. Or the new employee who asks him for assistance in figuring out how to use the company's phone system. But real, you know, customers! People who pay Johnson's some money in return for goods and services. Specifically, Ron talks to a number of customers who have placed those notorious rush* orders with Johnson's. And he finds out some interesting things.]

RON: We'd been getting all tangled up in our own accounting systems trying to figure out who ought to eat the cost for the rush orders. Should they be charged to the Service Center? Charged to the stores? Consolidated under some sort of corporate goodwill or marketing account? We forgot to even consider that maybe nobody would have to "eat" the cost. Maybe the customer would be willing to pay it. You know what they all said when I asked them? They said: "I'm in there at the last minute trying to get clothes to wear to my wedding, which is just a couple of days away. You think I'm going to be concerned about an extra twenty-five or thirty bucks? So long as it's within reason, I'll pay it. And thirty bucks ain't so bad. I understand the way things work—you want special service, you expect to pay. What's wrong with that?" That's what they all told me. Only the trick was remembering to ask them first.

ART: At first I was a little nervous about asking people for extra money for the overnight service. People come in here in a situation like that, they've already got a lot on their mind, to say the least. Then I'm supposed to hit them with a $30 rush charge. That's a little shaky to me. Then somebody comes up with a terrific idea. We reset our pricing structure. The basic price includes all those extra costs built in—overtime, overnight delivery, and all the rest. But then we say: "If you place your order more than seventy-two hours before delivery, we'll give you a $30 discount. If you place the order two weeks before the delivery date, we'll give you another 10 percent off. And if you place the order three months before delivery, that's another 10 percent off." That gives the customer an incentive to get in here early. It's good for us—helps us run the business more smoothly. We can pass the saving on to the customer. And we don't have to hit him with a surcharge when he comes in. Terrific idea. Know whose it was? Ellen's. I was at the Service Center a couple of weeks ago having a cup of coffee with her.

Mentioned to her how tough it was to hit the customer up for the $30 shipping charge, and boom! She lays out this whole pricing structure idea. We checked it out in headquarters, tried it out in a couple of stores, and it worked so well that it's now company policy. All Ellen's idea.

ELLEN: Yes, we still get rush orders, and we still go into a sort of "scramble mode" when one comes in. But now we also have some more resources in place to deliver that extra service. We can afford those resources because of the price differential. We're also seeing that the average order is being placed significantly earlier than it used to be. Customers have an incentive to come in early, so they do. As a result, the efficiency of the operation at the Service Center has improved dramatically. Things just go much, much more smoothly. They work better. It's a more pleasant place to work. People are happier. Our customers are happier, which is all that really matters. And that makes me feel good. Even though I may not see our customers every day, I know they're why I'm here. My people know that, too. I make sure of it. And when our customers are happy, we're happy.

QUIZ
Johnson's Formal Wear

1. From the perspective of Ellen Wojzahowicz, which scenario yielded the best results and why?
   a. Scenario A, because it served to remind her of the innately more important role played by the stores than by the Service Center—and where does she get off complaining about things, anyway?
   b. Scenario B, because it enabled the Service Center personnel to play their "let's make arbitrary changes to our order acceptance standards just to keep the stores on their toes" practical jokes, and that was good for the morale of Ellen's troops.

    c. Scenario C, because Johnson's customers were happy to have received the value for which they had paid, and in the long run that's what is best for Ellen.

2. From the perspective of Art Paine, which scenario yielded the best results and why?
    a. Scenario A, because it enabled the store personnel to play their "let's send in a fake rush order to the Service Center at 11:00 P.M. on New Year's Eve" practical jokes, and that was good for the morale of Art's troops.
    b. Scenario B, because it enabled one of his store managers to sharpen her administrative skills to such a point that she won a gold medal in the most recent Bureaucrats' Olympics for a paper entitled "Collecting, Analyzing, and Disseminating Copious Amounts of Store Traffic and Sales Data for No Particular Reason."
    c. Scenario C, because Johnson's customers were happy to have received the value for which they had paid, and in the long run that's what is best for Art.

3. From the perspective of Ron Robinson, which scenario yielded the best results and why?
    a. Scenario A, because it made fifty-three store managers happy and just one Service Center manager unhappy, and he could live with those odds.
    b. Scenario B, because it satisfied the Service Center manager, who worked in the same building he did, and he figured he could live with the irate phone calls from the store managers, who were spread out all over the state.
    c. Scenario C, because Johnson's customers were happy to have received the value for which they had paid, and in the long run that's what is best for Ron.

4. From the perspective of Johnson's Formal Wear, which scenario yielded the best results and why?
    a. Scenario A, because it provided the kind of structural tension necessary to hold a complex organization together in today's dynamic and challenging business world.

    b. Scenario B, because it provided the kind of structural tension necessary to hold a complex organization together in today's dynamic and challenging business world.

    c. Scenario C, because Johnson's customers were happy to have received the value for which they had paid, and in the long run that's what is best for Johnson's.

5. From the perspective of a typical Johnson's customer, which scenario yielded the best results and why?

    a. Scenario A, because the increased level of chaos at the Service Center would increase the chances that the suit the customer eventually got wouldn't fit, and that would be good for a laugh at his wedding.

    b. Scenario B, because anybody who decides to get married on forty-eight hours' notice probably wouldn't mind a hurdle or two being put in his way.

    c. Scenario C, because receiving the value for which they've paid is really all that customers care about.

The Big Game!

Football has become as important a part of the American fall ritual as back-to-school sales, political campaigns, and marital discord caused by one spouse's insistence on making a 300-mile trip across bad, narrow roads in heavy traffic in order to drink cider and see leaves. And as exciting as the end of the football season can be, what with bowl games and playoff games (not to mention leaves safely covered by snow), there is something extra special about the first game of the year. New faces . . . new hope . . . a new remote control unit for the TV so that you can follow three or four games at once without having to rearrange the pillows on the couch every time you get up to change channels. Well, opening day for the new QFL—the Quality Football League—is no exception. Attention is focused on the gridiron conflict looming on the horizon [Editor's note: when people write about football, they must be allowed to use phrases like "gridiron conflict loom-ing on the horizon"], which will pit the QFL's two flagship franchises, the Pittsburgh Pillagers and the Oklahoma City Obsessive-Compulsives (also known as the OC OC's).

You couldn't make these two teams more different if you tied a pack mule to a corral gate with mesquite shavings. (If that doesn't make any sense to you, you need to do some boning up on good-ol'-boy football lingo.) And the differences in the team are paralleled by the differences in their head coaches. The Pittsburgh Pillagers are led by legendary mentor Hack Krump. He needs no introduction to true football fans, who probably best remember him from the time he tore an opponent's arm off at the shoulder and then used the enemy appendage to block a would-be game-winning field goal in the closing seconds of the NFL's 1953 championship game. About all you need to know to understand Hack's approach to the game is that the license plate on his battered, rusted out four-wheel-drive vehicle reads JES WHUP 'EM!

Leading the OC's into battle is a far less well-known X-and-O man, F. Murray LaMont, Ph.D. Dr. LaMont, known to his friends as "Dr. LaMont," is a clinical psychologist specializing in Advanced Obfuscation and Solipsism. Relatively new to the parlance of pigskin peregrinations, Dr. LaMont has applied himself with the diligence for which he hopes to someday become noted. He has spent countless late-night hours hud-dled with his coaches, asking such penetrating questions as "How many on a side?" "Where does this infield-fly-rule thing come in?" and "Really, though—why *do* you suppose the players pat each other on the fanny like that?"

Central to the OC's championship quest will be the appli-cation of what is known as the "internal customer" model of quality. As Dr. LaMont said in a recent interview published in *Grunt!*, the official magazine of the QFL: "What we're after is the quality execution of quality football plays by quality foot-ball players. The internal customer model provides the kind of intellectual and analytical framework onto which we can hang the quasi-independent variable indices of success. Beat Pittsburgh!"

As game time approaches, the two teams wait anxiously in their locker rooms. If the opening game of the season has a special importance, then the last few moments before that opening game take on an added significance. Because it's in those moments that the respective head coaches—Krump for the Pillagers, Dr. LaMont for the OC's—have a chance to set the tone for the helmeted hellaciousness ahead, and in the process to dramatically affect their charges' search for shoulder-padded supremacy. Let's go into the locker rooms and listen to what the two field commanders have to say.

Dr. LaMont's Pregame Pep Talk to the OC's

Men, in a few minutes, we're going to get out there, buckle up those chin straps, put on our game faces— Of course, you'd probably want to put on your game face *before* you buckle up the chin strap, but then, it's just a figure of speech—well, actually a metaphor—so I don't suppose you take it literally anyway, so never mind. Anyway, we're going to go out there and do our dead-level darndest to play a quality game of football. You know what that means, don't you? It means taking a *process-intensive approach* to the game! And you know how we're going to do that, don't you? We're going to do it by making sure we perform each piece of the process in a way that is of quality to our *internal customers!* So let's review some of the important things we've been working on all week.

Benvenuti—you're the quarterback. Everybody else on this team is looking to you for leadership and inspiration. In other words, these other forty-four guys are your customers! So is the coaching staff, because we're looking to you to deliver skillful execution of the strategies that we've developed over the week. So we're your customers, too. And the officials, don't forget about them. Because sometimes, I'm told, the play can get a little rough out there on that field, and when it does, those men in the striped shirts need to be able to count on cooler heads to prevail, and that means you. Although actually, they'd probably be more inclined to come to *me* to try to get things straightened out, and then I would come to you. So that makes me your customer—of course, we've already covered that—or would you be my customer? And then you'd be more of a subcontractor for the officials than a customer. And I guess I'm a customer of the officials and a value-added reseller as far as you're concerned, since I'll take what the official tells me and pass it along to you, adding value in the form of clarity and motivational content. And don't forget the little people up in the stands. The folks who sell the beer and the hot dogs. They're counting on you to give them an exciting game, because it's when the fans get excited that they yell a lot, and it's when they yell a lot that they buy a lot of beer, and that's what the beer sellers are looking for—so they're your customers, too. Is that clear?

Horowitz—you're the center. Benvenuti is counting on you to give him a good, clean snap of the ball on every play. So he's your customer. Of course, since everyone on the team is Benvenuti's customer, that makes you his customer, too. So I guess what the two of you really have going is more like a partnership. Maybe a joint venture. Whatever. Don't you forget it!

And the rest of you offensive linemen! You've got to protect Benvenuti. And you've got to open up those holes that will let our running backs like Fulton and Doubleday make those big gains. So you've got a couple of different sets of customers. You're really serving two markets—the quarterback market and the running back market. And depending on how finely you want to sort things, you've got two segments within the running back market—halfbacks and fullbacks. I really don't think you want to slice things any finer than that, or you might get a little confused. Just keep those primary market segmentations in mind and you'll do just fine.

Drew, the tight end! Listen up! You're really part of the down-blocking process, so that means you need to be a finely tuned part of the offensive line. Those other guys are counting on you. They're your customers! And since those Pillagers like to do a lot of strong side blitzing out of the nickel set, you've gotta deliver some strong protection to Benvenuti, too. Of course, he's gotta deliver you the ball when you get open on those crossing routes, so you're his customer as well. And don't you forget it, Benvenuti! And, Drew, I suppose the tackle on your side of the line has got to be able to pick up the slack when you got out on those patterns, so that makes you his customer as well. So the best I can figure it, you're pretty much everybody's customer and everybody is also your customer. Kind of like an interlocking directorate. So lay low, or the zebras might not like the looks of that.

"Now Pzzrszzki, the place kicker. Be sure to remember how all of this works out for you. Grusheski, the long snapper, and La-Mont, Jr., the backup quarterback and holder, are certainly your suppliers, and you're their customer. Of course, all forty-four guys are your customers, too, seeing as how they're going to be out there getting beat up for sixty minutes, and if the game comes down to a field goal, I think it's safe to say that they're going to be counting on you, and they'll be kind of p.o.'d if they lose on account of a guy who hasn't broken a sweat since he left his job at the rake factory in the old country. You got that? Now, when it comes to kickoffs, I suppose it depends on whether it's a deep kick or an on-side kick. If it's a deep kick— What's that? The game's about to start? They want us out on the field?

Well, men. I guess we don't have time to do any more last-minute preparation and motivation. So this is it. But there is one final thing I want to say to all of you before you get out there. I want you to remember the words of the immortal coach Vic Lombardi— Whuzzat? Vince? Apparently it's *Vince* Lombardi. Anyway, when things get tough out there on that field for you this afternoon—and at some point, they will—I want you to remember these words: "When the going gets tough, the tough remember to serve their internal customer!"

Beat Pittsburgh!

Hack Krump's Pep Talk to the Pillagers

Let's get the %#!@$ out there and kick some %#!@$*& OC ass!

Postscript

Final score:

Pillagers	56
OC's	0

I Lost the Internal Customer of My Heart to the External Supplier of Her Love (Quality Song of the Year: Country & Western Division)

Well I always thought our love was special,
I always thought that it would never end.
I know that my approach was intellect'ul,
But I didn't think it'd drive her 'round the bend.

She was the internal customer of my heart.
I've loved her for all these years.
She's with the external supplier of her love,
Now I'm cryin' external tears.

I shoulda seen the clues—God knows she left some,
Maybe then she'd still be here, right by me.
Course, shootin' my dog ain't 'xactly what I'd call subtle,
But I guess my love was blind as blind can be.

She was the internal customer of my heart.
Just the memory's what remains.
She's with the external supplier of her love.
Now I'm feelin' internal pains.

She never did quite understand the process
By which she knew that I'd always be there.
Now she has a warehouse full of slap and tickle,
And not a just-in-time supply of love and care.

She was the internal customer of my heart.
I wanted to make her my wife.
She's with the external supplier of her love,
And they've put a quality stop on my life.

The Paradoxes
of Quality

The institutions of the new pluralism have no purpose except outside of themselves. They exist in contemplation of a "customer" or a "market." Achievement in the hospital is not a satisfied nurse, but a cured *former* patient. Achievement in business is not a happy work force, however desirable it may be; it is a satisfied customer who reorders the product. (Peter F. Drucker, *The Frontiers of Management*, p. 175)

* * *

As usual, Peter Drucker has insightful things to say; as usual, he says them most eloquently. In fact, he has summarized in a few dozen words what we have been discussing in these past 211 pages. Because what this book is about is not the techniques of quality improvement but the fundamental connectedness of quality and customer satisfaction. Not the "how" of quality, but the "why."

It's my guess that there is virtually nothing said in this book that you didn't already know. What's at issue here is perspective, a way of looking at things, however basic they might be:

- That the customer is the final arbiter when it comes to quality.
- That the customer's perspective on things is necessarily different from the supplier's perspective.
- That the customer is paying the supplier to worry about the details.
- That the customer's decisions are based on impressions, and that those impressions are the relevant reality.
- That customers form impressions surrounding every aspect of doing business—not just about the products or services but about the total transaction.
- That customers are seeking "the most for their money," i.e., value.

Not only do we know those things intellectually, we know them viscerally. We feel them dozens of times every day in our capacity as the customer of the local supermarket, gas station, computer vendor, physician, government agency, restaurant, you name it.

So why is it so bloody difficult? Why are quality objectives so tough to achieve? Let me suggest two reasons, one philosophical, the other pragmatic.

On a philosophical level, the issue is how to be part of an organization that is "special" or "different." The word often used these days is "excellence": excelling, standing out from the crowd. Now, everyone ought to strive for excellence. That much is clear. But—and here's the rub—everyone *can't* be excellent. Everyone *can't* stand out from the crowd; if that's where everyone is, then that *is* the crowd.

The more pragmatic reason is that the task of achieving quality is too straightforward. It isn't complicated enough. That's Quality Paradox Number One. Sounds crazy, but I think it's true. We like to think that we get paid for being smart and clever, for our ability to think and sort out and sift through and solve complex problems. We don't get paid for "heavy lifting," or if we do, we aspire to a position where we don't. Call it the "I don't do windows" syndrome.

Well, quality isn't complex. But it is hard. Hard as hell. Quality is precisely about windows and heavy lifting. It's precisely about the details. It's precisely about treating customers—*people*—the way we'd like to be treated. It's precisely about making sure that those customers—those *people*—get what they paid for. That's as straightforward as it gets, and should we forget it, we can be sure we'll be reminded of it—of what it's like to be the customer—dozens of times today, and then again tomorrow, and then again the next day.

We are conditioned to think a certain way at work and often strive to be perceived as practical, nuts-and-bolts, hands-on guys (with the word "guys" here describing an attitude, not a gender). In my work, I have the opportunity to give a lot of talks on the general topic of "viewing quality from the customer's perspective." Those talks are customarily followed by a question-and-answer session. And those sessions are customarily led off with a question of the form: "I understand what you're saying about the necessity of delivering value to the customer as a theoretical matter, and I endorse it wholeheartedly. But now let's get practical. Can you give me five things I can do tomorrow to begin to implement some of these ideas?" That question is from the membership creed of the Society of Nuts-and-Bolts Guys. I mean, how can you get more practical and responsible than that: "Theory's good. Real world's better. Let's do it."

It's also the toughest question that I face. Not because I can't offer such suggestions. Quite the opposite. It's because if you really do "understand . . . the necessity of delivering value to the customer as a theoretical matter," then you would necessarily realize that seeing quality from the customer's perspective involves nothing less than:

- Changing the mind set of an entire organization, so that all employees in that organization come to grips with one fundamental truth—that this organization exists to deliver value to its customers.
- Making sure that all employees—all departments, all functions, all levels—understand the direct connection between

the tasks they're performing and the value received by the customer.

- Taking whatever steps are necessary to ensure that those connections to the customer are clearly made and constantly reinforced through compensation systems, communications systems, recognition systems, new employee orientation, training, whatever.
- Never letting up; never being satisfied.

If you truly understand that that is the issue at hand, then I contend that it's impossible to see it as a theoretical as opposed to practical matter—that it's impossible not to see five *hundred* things you can do "tomorrow" to begin to implement these ideas. (In the interest of trying to practice what I preach, I should acknowledge that I'm not about to "blame" my customers—the people to whom I give such talks—for not understanding. I fully accept the notion that "if the student didn't learn, then the teacher didn't teach," and that it's my responsibility to look for ways to try to make my case more clearly and more effectively.)

So perhaps people don't understand the issue as well as they think they do. But there's another possibility and, frankly, I think it's far more likely. Namely, that people *do* understand the true nature of the problem, that more people understand it every day, and as the implications of the real issue at hand begin to sink in, they look for ways to put off the necessity of coming to grips with that issue. It's a little like having a load of gravel dumped in your driveway. The gravel is for a new drainage ditch you're digging in your back yard. You would like to have had the load dumped right next to the site for the ditch, but try as you might, you can't figure out a way to get the truck into the back yard without uprooting hedges or disassembling the guest room. You spend hours devising this or that clever scheme. But at some point the solution will hit you, and it will involve a shovel and a wheelbarrow and sweat. And that's more than a little daunting.

Quality is like that. It *means* heavy lifting. It *means* attention to detail. It *means* looking at things from the customer's perspective. It *means* making sure that customers feel the way we like to feel when we're the customer. It *means* always accepting the customer's input as, if not necessarily right, then necessarily valid. Complex? No. Hard? There is nothing harder. At one point in my career, I was given responsibility for running a "Customer Satisfaction Tracking Survey" for my company. Every quarter, one-fourth of the company's customers were sent a lengthy, detailed survey designed to give us feedback on all aspects of doing business with us. The company made very complex, very high-technology systems to be used in a production environment. That meant that the operation of those systems had to be explained in a very clear, thorough way; documentation—the manuals which described system use and maintenance—was a nontrivial matter. Invariably, alas, the lowest-rated area of customer satisfaction was "documentation."

After two consecutive quarters of poor ratings for documentation, we convened a meeting to discuss what could be done to resolve the issue. Five or six of us sat around a conference table, wracking our brains to uncover the "secret."

"Maybe," suggested one person, "what we're dealing with here is that the sales rep isn't doing a good job of explaining the documentation to the customer, so the customer isn't quite sure of how to use it. Maybe it's a sales problem."

"Are we sure that the customer has bright enough people trying to use the documentation?" someone else offered. "I don't mean that the people are dumb, but maybe they haven't been properly trained. Maybe it's a training issue."

I chimed in with my theory. "It could be that what we're seeing is the result of last-minute changes in the product design," I said. "The documentation people have to begin writing these things almost a year before the product is delivered. If engineering makes a late design change, there's no way it will be reflected in the manual. Maybe that's the cause of the problem."

The meeting seemed to be going well. I was delighted. A lot of ideas were being generated, areas to explore being identified. Each was more clever than the last—but then, wasn't that what we were being paid for? Our smarts, right?

Then somebody came up with a truly revolutionary idea. "Maybe," he said, "these low ratings for documentation mean that our documentation stinks." And when he said that, there was a sort of stunned silence. Then we all looked at each other. Then we all laughed.

In our efforts to sort out what our customers really meant, we were ignoring what they were telling us. We were looking for "the secret." The only trouble was that our customers weren't keeping any secrets from us. They had told us: "Your documentation stinks." Here we had gone to the time and trouble and expense of asking our customers to identify problem areas—we had "done it right": gotten "close to the customer"—and yet our reflexive response was to assume that, since after all we were the "experts," we must impose our interpretation onto what our customers were telling us.

There is a word for that behavior. The word is "arrogance," and it was the result of forgetting that even though we may have been the experts when it came to running our business, our customers were the experts when it came to quality. None of this is to say that some of our more arcane solutions might not have had some validity. In fact, some did. Rather, it's a caution not to make things any more complex than they have to be, not to outsmart yourself.

Quality isn't complex. It *is* very hard, and the reason it's so hard is that it involves not so much changing what we do as changing how we think. Not so much figuring out how to achieve quality as coming to grips with the fact that we already know how and now it's a matter of getting down and doing it—windows, heavy lifting, and all. This book is not about quality techniques, but about how to apply those proven, powerful techniques—about how to frame the issue at hand. And that leads us to Quality Paradox Number Two: If our objective is quality, we won't achieve it. The way to achieve quality is by striving to deliver value to the customer.

That, I think, is ultimately the lesson that we must learn,

the way the quality issue must be framed. Boldly, cleanly, clearly. It means applying all the lessons gained from a lifetime's experience as customers and not being afraid to be perhaps just a notch less "expert" on the job. It means standing back from all the details of organizational life—the details that the customer pays us to deal with—and seeing things from the customer's perspective. It means coming to grips with the fact that we know what needs to be done and then just . . . doing it.

I began this discussion with a quote from Peter Drucker. It seems a sensible way to end it, as well:

> A favorite story at management meetings is that of the three stonecutters who were asked what they were doing. The first replied: "I am making a living." The second kept on hammering while he said: "I am doing the best job of stonecutting in the entire country." The third one looked up with a visionary gleam in his eyes and said: "I am building a cathedral."
>
> The third man is, of course, the true "manager." The first man knows what he wants to get out of the work and manages to do so. He is likely to give a "fair day's work for a fair day's pay." But he is not a manager and will never be one.
>
> It is the second man who is a problem. Workmanship is essential, without it no work can flourish; in fact, an organization demoralizes if it does not demand of its members the most scrupulous workmanship they are capable of. But there is always a danger that the true workman, the true professional, will believe that he is accomplishing something when in effect he is just polishing stones or collecting footnotes. Workmanship must be encouraged in the business enterprise. But it must always be related to the needs of the whole. (Drucker, *The Practice of Management*, p. 122)

Although Drucker is speaking in the context of effective management, it's a lesson that can be applied—a mind set that can be adopted—by anyone: management or rank and file, line or staff function, publicly traded company or not-for-profit organization, private business or government agency. Yes, workmanship is essential, and the application of any available techniques to improve the level of workmanship should—must—be embraced. But in the process—and quality is, after all, a process issue—don't lose sight of the broader perspective. Yes, you're cutting stones; that's the "what." But you're also building a cathedral; that's the "why." Yes, you're "doing a job." But in so doing, you're helping to create something of value for your customers.

That's the objective. The way to frame the issue. The "why" of quality. The opportunities are there for you. All that's left for you to do is to take them.

It Doesn't Take Much

Our friend Ben Dalton finally has his dream house in order and has installed an alarm system that works. He has just returned from a business trip, one aspect of which he found memorable:

First of all, I wasn't too thrilled about the fact that I had to fly out on a Sunday afternoon. I'm away from Marcia and the kids often enough without having to cut into my weekends, too. But I really didn't have a choice, and when you gotta go, you gotta go.

As it turned out, there were no direct flights to Atlanta, which seemed strange, since when I'm *not* trying to go to Atlanta, every flight I take has to stop there. Anyway, I had to make a connection in New York. We were scheduled to leave at 1:30 and arrive in New York at 3:00. My flight to Atlanta was at 4:00. So I had one hour to make the connection. Not great, not bad.

I get to the airport, to the gate, at 12:50. It's about 90 degrees— I'm talking about inside the building, at the gate. I ask the ticket agent: "Isn't it a little hot in here?" He says: "It sure is." I say: "Well, can't you do something about it?" He says: "Like what?" I go back and sit down. And sweat.

At 1:15 the flight begins boarding. Ever notice how rows 25 through 30 are boarded first, but about 150 people get up and get on the plane? The rows must be wider in the back. Anyway, we're all on the plane for our 1:30 flight. It's 1:40, and we're still at the gate; 1:45—still at the gate; 1:50—still at the gate. No announcements. No apologies. No explanations. No nothing.

Then the guy sitting next to me—he's at a window seat, I'm in an aisle seat—looks out the window and says: "Oh, oh." He points out the window. I look. There are three guys standing under the wing looking up. Then a fourth guy comes out to join them, and now I know we're in real trouble because he's got a tie on.

By now it's almost two o'clock. The little bridge game under the wing has broken up, but still no word about the delay. Then, finally, at about 2:10, somebody comes on the intercom: "We regret to announce that because of a mechanical problem, we must use substitute equipment." It took me a minute to realize that "equipment" meant "airplane" and not a set of socket wrenches. So we had to get off the plane, which took about ten minutes, march over to a new gate, and get on another plane, which took another ten minutes.

So now it's 2:30, and my 1:30 flight is just about to leave. Being aces in arithmetic, I figure that my comfortable one-hour connection is going to be a little on the tight side. We take off at 2:33 and—finally a little bit of good luck—we happen to catch a pretty good tailwind, which gets us into New York at about 3:50. So I've got ten minutes to get to my connecting flight.

Naturally, there's no agent waiting with gate information. So I go looking for a monitor. Not one in sight. Then it dawns on me. We're in this auxiliary terminal, not the main terminal for this airline. Mind you, there are no signs telling me this. I just realized it because I had been through that terminal once before, and I remembered that you had to get a shuttle bus over to the main terminal.

I figure it cost me two, three minutes wandering around, which doesn't sound like a lot until you realize that I only had ten minutes to begin with. I go up to somebody who looks like an employee of the airline and I ask him: "Where do I get the bus over to the main terminal?" It seemed like all he could do to nod his head down a corridor. I'm a little exasperated, so I say: "Don't you suppose a couple of signs would be nice?" He shrugs. I run down the corridor.

I get out to the curb. It looks like the right place, but there still aren't any signs. I ask somebody else from the airline: "Is this where I get the bus to the main terminal? He nods. Are they all required to take a vow of silence now?

The bus pulls up. It's 3:57. The door opens. I get on and say to the driver: "I've got a 4:00 flight to Atlanta. Any chance I'm going to make it?" He says: "You are now." Then he closes the door behind me. There was nobody else waiting to get on. I'm the only one on the bus.

Well, he just hauls this thing through the traffic. You know how orderly traffic is around airline terminals, where cars and buses and cabs are triple-parked and all. Somehow he gets us to the curb. He opens the door of the bus, scrambles off in front of me, and shouts back over his shoulder: "Follow me!"

I follow him into the terminal, and he runs interference for me through the crowds at the baggage claims area. The bus driver! And his bus is still running, empty, out front! He stops for about five seconds in front of a monitor. Then he leads me over to an escalator and says: "Go up this escalator, take a left. Go through security, and your gate's right there." I fumble in my pocket for a buck, give it to him, thank him, and run to my gate. It was right where he said it was. Made it with about a minute to spare.

It was the damndest thing. I mean, everything about that flight was a disaster. The overheated terminal. The unexplained delay. Changing "equipment." The confusion at the auxiliary terminal. The airline personnel who made me feel like I was imposing on them to tell me where the bus was. All of that was rotten. But do you know what I remember about that flight? Yeah. The bus driver. He made me feel like I was being taken care of. I came away with pleasant thoughts about that flight—when I think about it, even about that airline. I know that sounds strange but it's true. All because of the bus driver. And I gave him a buck. A buck! Hell, I'd like to adopt him. But that probably wouldn't work out. He was fifty-five, sixty years old.

You know, the pity of it is that it doesn't take much to keep people happy. You'd think more businesses would realize that, but they don't.

QUIZ
"It Doesn't Take Much"

1. Why didn't the ticket agent do anything about the excessive temperature at the gate?
   a. He was hypothermic, so he liked it.
   b. He assumed it was all part of the airline's new Frequent Perspirers Program.
   c. He didn't like Ben Dalton's attitude.
   d. He didn't see it as his job.

2. Why didn't the airline at least acknowledge the delay in the departure of Ben's flight?
   a. What delay?
   b. Airline companies measure delays with calendars, not clocks.
   c. The airline didn't like Ben Dalton's attitude.
   d. Nobody saw it as his job.

3. What were the three men discussing under the wing?
   a. How hot it was inside the terminal.
   b. The need for new equipment.
   c. Ben Dalton's attitude.
   d. Whose job it was to go get the guy with the tie.

4. Who was the guy with the tie?
   a. The guy with the authority to cancel the flight.
   b. The guy who could fix the equipment.
   c. The guy who could fix the air conditioning in the terminal.
   d. The guy who knew where the ON button was for the airplane's intercom.

5. Why weren't there any signs in the auxiliary terminal directing people to the main terminal?
   a. Because anybody important wouldn't be flying into an auxiliary terminal so what difference does it make?
   b. It was part of the airline's new "Frequent Walking Around in Circles Wondering What to Do Next" program.
   c. Ben's attitude. The signs were put back up just as soon as he was gone.
   d. The guy with the tie told them not to bother.

6. Why did the bus driver treat Ben so well?
   a. It was his first week working for the airline so he didn't realize that providing such service wasn't his job.
   b. He just didn't understand the complexities of the business world.
   c. A retiree who had been CEO of his own company up until a few months ago, he knew what business

travel was like and wanted to do what he could to help.

    d. He liked Ben's "never say die" attitude.

7. What's the real lesson in all this?

    a. "Equipment" really means "airplane."

    b. Ben's got an attitude problem.

    c. Little things mean a lot.

    d. Anybody can make a difference.

You, Your Customers,
and Quality: The Fundamentals

They have the money, you want it.
They have the perception, you cause it.
You know what it's like, you've lived it.
You know what needs doing, so do it.